LAKE VILLA DISTRICT LIBRARY
3 1981 00404 1764

MY SWEET VEGAN
passionate about dessert

by Hannah Kaminsky

D1529717

LAKE VILLA DISTRICT LIBRARY
1001 EAST GRAND AVENUE
LAKE VILLA, IL 60046
(847) 356-7711

Content Text Copyright © 2007 by Hannah Kaminsky
Photographs Copyright © 2007 by Hannah Kaminsky

Author Portrait by Autumn Photography
Cover Text by Alisa Fleming
Designed by Andrea Schaaf

All rights reserved. No part of this book may be reproduced or transmitted in any form or by any means, electronic or mechanical, including photocopying, recording, or by an information storage retrieval system without written permission from the publisher.

ISBN-10 0-9791286-1-7
ISBN-13 978-0-9791286-1-5

Printed in Thailand

Published by Fleming Ink
Henderson, Nevada

www.flemingink.com

Thank You!

Yes, you, reading this book! Without a considerate audience, which includes people like you, I wouldn't even be able to dream of having the opportunity to put my recipes into print. That is why I want to thank you, first and foremost, for your interest, kindness, and open mind.

Of course, there are so many people whose dedication and hard work made all of this possible, and to them I truly owe the world. My parents deserve an award for their persistence, never giving up, even when I did. I wish I had more than just words to show how much I appreciate their own personal struggles to provide me with the best in life, not to mention all of the dirty dishes that they had to put up with throughout this whole project.

Additionally, kudos should definitely go to all of my friends and family who tasted and reviewed such a myriad of baked goods. Just thinking about it makes my head spin! Thank you guys for all of the encouragement when you thought I got it right, and for suffering through the rejected recipes, too.

And where would I be without Alisa, my wonderful publisher? I still can't believe my luck that you saw a book in me. All of the logistics aside, you and Anthony really went above and beyond the call of duty, putting in countless hours for revisions, brainstorming, and labor; every single minute of your time was absolutely irreplaceable.

Last but not least, I want to give a big shout out to all of the amazingly talented bloggers out there who continue to inspire me. If not for your shining examples, I would never have even begun to share my creations with the world.

–Hannah

Table of Contents

Cakes and Cupcakes

Pies and Tarts

88

112

142

Miscellaneous Morsels and Desserts

170

Introduction

Writing my own cookbook has long been a dream of mine. The title My Sweet Vegan was swimming around in my head long before my first cookbook-worthy recipe was ever developed. Yet to have this book become a reality at the mere age of eighteen feels completely surreal.

Based on my earliest ventures in the kitchen as a new vegan and young adolescent, even I could have been convinced that eggs and dairy really are indispensable to delectable sweets. During my freshman year in high school I churned out muffins and cookies more akin to cement doorstops than desserts, but I never gave up. I was adamant that my creations would one day taste better than the pre-packaged and non-vegan options on the market. For that matter, it was unacceptable in my eyes to serve a good vegan pastry; it needed to be delicious by anyone's standards.

As you might imagine, my solo kitchen escapades have been filled with many trials and countless errors. Oh boy... I remember the first time I tried to make vegan marshmallows. It was, quite possibly my largest, and definitely stickiest, explosion to date. I'm not talking about a trivial spraying of the walls; marshmallow goop was all over the floor, stove, stuck inside door handles, dripping into drawers, in my hair, the whole nine yards.

Yet, through these spectacular failures, near meltdowns, painful burns, and piles of dirty dishes I have learned, quite simply, what works and what doesn't. Reworking recipes four, five, even six times, I have gradually unlocked the "secrets" to vegan baking, to produce mouthwatering delights that appeal to everyone.

After winning two bake-off awards, I bolstered up the nerve to venture outside of my comfort zone, and make my "international debut." Over a year ago, I launched my first blog, Bittersweet. Bittersweet has been an irreplaceable outlet for my crafting, photography, and of course baking. Updated almost obsessively, I post nearly every day about the various things that I knit, crochet, sew, bead, photograph, or cook. Please do stop in and visit me at bittersweetblog.wordpress.com when you get the chance.

Four years have now passed since I first became a vegan, and I am once again preparing for my freshman year, but this time in university. While my primary motivation for creating this cookbook was to share my tried and true recipes with as many people as possible, I certainly wouldn't complain if it helps with the college loans I am sorely anticipating... and maybe even allows for a few extra indulgences, like some really good vanilla beans.

Whether you are vegan, have food allergies, or are just looking for some great dessert ideas, I truly hope that you enjoy every recipe in my first cookbook. Happy Baking!

Ingredient Guide

Vegan living opens up a whole new world of fascinating and delicious natural ingredients that many unadventurous eaters might never even have the pleasure of trying. While some of these foods may have been considered quite obscure in the past, they are quickly making their way into the mainstream, thanks to the advent of the Internet. Most if not all of the ingredients listed below are available to purchase online, should they not be found in your local area.

Agave Nectar

Derived from the same plant as tequila but far less potent, agave is the sweet syrup at the core of cacti. It is available in both light and dark varieties; the dark possesses a greater intensity, while the light more closely resembles honey in flavor. Unrefined, agave nectar has a much lower glycemic index than many traditional sweeteners, and is therefore consumed by some diabetics in moderation. Any health food or natural food store worth its stuff should readily stock agave nectar.

Agar (Agar-Agar)

Known also as kanten, agar is a gelatinous substance made out of seaweed. It is a perfect substitute for traditional gelatin, which is extracted from the collagen within animals' connective tissues and obviously very non-vegan. Agar comes in both powdered and flaked form. I prefer to use the powder because it is more concentrated and measures gram for gram like standard gelatin. However, if you can only find the flakes, just whiz them in a spice grinder for a few minutes and —viola, instant agar powder! Agar can be found in Asian markets and some health food stores.

All-Purpose Flour

While wonderful flours can be made from all sorts of grains and beans, the gold standard in everyday baking would be all-purpose. Falling somewhere between cake flour and bread flour, all-purpose flour has the ability to create light desserts that still have substance. It is therefore used most often in my recipes, and stocked as one of my pantry staples. All-purpose flour may be labeled in stores as unbleached white flour or simply "plain flour."

Almond Meal/Flour

Almond flour is simply the end result of grinding down raw almonds into a coarse powder. To make your own, just throw a pound or so of completely unadulterated almonds into your food processor, and let the machine work its magic. If you opt to stock up and save some for later, be sure to store the freshly ground almond flour within an airtight container in the refrigerator or freezer. Due to their high oil content, ground nuts can go rancid fairly quickly. To cut down on labor and save a little time, almond flour can be purchased in bulk from natural food grocers, and is often labeled as almond meal.

Apple Cider Vinegar

As with oil, vinegar may originate from different types of produce, and the flavor will vary depending upon the source. Thinking along these lines, apple cider vinegar could be considered the olive oil of vinegars; flavorful, useful, and an all-around great thing to have on hand. Regular white wine vinegar or the other standard options would certainly work, but the distinctive flavor of apple cider vinegar rounds out baked goods so perfectly, and it is so easy to find... why wouldn't you use it? Hunt around the oil and salad dressing aisles in your local supermarket, where you should have no problem finding it.

Arrowroot Powder/Flour

Thanks to arrowroot you can thicken sauces, puddings and mousses with ease. This white powder is very similar to kudzu and is often compared to other starchy flours. However, arrowroot is so fine that it produces much smoother results, and is less likely to stick together and form large, glutinous lumps when baking. In a pinch, cornstarch can be an adequate substitute, but I highly recommend seeking out arrowroot. Most mega-marts have a brand or two tucked in among the spices in the baking aisle.

Black Cocoa Powder

What do you get when you oxidize Dutch process cocoa powder to the extreme? Black cocoa, of course! Dark as coal, it certainly lives up to its name and produces amazing color in baked goods. However, it has a much lower fat content than standard cocoa, and should therefore be used sparingly to avoid altering the texture of your baked goods. I rarely use black cocoa, because it is difficult to find and more expensive than the alternative. Nonetheless, if you wish to create breath-taking chocolate desserts, black cocoa will never fail to impress. You can hunt it down at some tea or spice specialty shops, but if all else fails, a search online should prove fruitful. Otherwise, feel free to substitute regular Dutch process cocoa for an equally tasty, if comparatively pale, dessert.

Brown Rice Syrup

Caramel-colored and thick like honey, brown rice syrup is a natural sweetener that is produced via the fermentation of brown rice. It is actually less sweet than granulated sugar, adding a wholesome complexity to baked goods. The deep flavor of brown rice syrup is best cast in supporting roles, complimenting other aspects of the dish without taking center stage. Brown rice syrup can be found in health food stores across the map, but corn syrup will make a suitable substitute, if you are unable to find it locally.

Chocolate

Why is this a special ingredient? Chocolate is chocolate, right? One would assume so, but many name brands that prefer quantity to quality would beg to differ. Obviously, white and milk chocolate are out of the picture, yet some dark and semi-sweet chocolates still don't make the vegan cut. Even those that claim to be "70% cacao solids, extra-special dark" may have milk solids or butterfat lurking within. Don't buy the hype or the filler! Stay vigilant and check labels for milk-based ingredients, as unadulterated chocolate is far superior.

Chocolate Crème-Filled Sandwich Cookies

As America's favorite cookie, it is no surprise that the Oreo® would come up sooner or later on this list. While the original Oreo® is now changing its ways to take out the trans-fats and animal products, there are many other options that are even more ethically acceptable. Newman's Own makes an excellent organic version that tastes just like the cookies you might remember from your childhood. Plus, along with some exciting flavor variations, Newman-O's (as they are called) can even be found in a wheat-free format! Any Oreo-like wafers with a vegan crème filling will do, so it is up to your own discretion as to which brand you would like to endorse.

Chocolate Wafer Cookie Crumbs

Essentially just flat, crunchy cocoa cookies, there are quite a few vegan options on the market. I typically use the Alphabet Cookies from Newman's Own, but plenty of other brands will work exactly the same. Just be sure to check the ingredient statement, and stay away from those that look soft or chewy. For a thrifty endeavor, you could also try baking your own at home! With your cookies ready, pulverize them into crumbs using a food processor, spice grinder, or a good old-fashioned rubber mallet, depending upon your mood.

Confectioner's Sugar

Otherwise known as powdered sugar, icing sugar, or 10x sugar, confectioner's sugar is a very finely ground version of standard white sugar. There are many vegan options on the market, so just keep your eyes open and you will likely find a good supply. Of course, you can make your own confectioner's sugar by powdering 1 cup of granulated sugar with 1 tablespoon of cornstarch in your food processor or spice grinder. Simply blend the sugar and cornstarch on the highest speed for about two minutes, allowing the dust to settle before opening your machine up, unless you want to inhale a cloud of sugar!

Cream of Tartar

Don't let the name fool you; cream of tartar has absolutely nothing to do with either cream or tartar sauce. It is actually created through the fermentation process that grapes must undergo in the production of wine. As a result, cream of tartar contributes a good deal of acid to recipes. Sometimes used as a stabilizer, it can create flavors similar to buttermilk or take the place of baking powder when combined with the right chemicals. Scope out the baking section of your local grocery store for this one; you may be surprised by how common cream of tartar really is.

Flavor Extracts

In most cases, I try to stay as far away from extracts as possible, because they are all too often artificial, insipid, and a poor replacement for the real thing. However, real vanilla and almond are my two main exceptions, as high quality extracts from the actual sources are readily available in most markets. Just make sure to avoid any bottles that contain sugar, corn syrup, colors, or stabilizers in addition to your flavor of choice. For some of the more unusual extracts called for in this book, such as anise or root beer, a well-stocked supermarket should be able to accommodate your needs. Nonetheless, if your search ends up unsuccessful, the Internet will never let you down.

Flax Seeds

Ground flax seeds make an excellent vegan egg-replacer when combined with water. One tablespoon of the whole seeds produces approximately 1½ tablespoons of the ground powder. While you can purchase pre-ground flax meal in many stores, I prefer to grind the flax seeds fresh for each recipe, as they tend to go rancid rather quickly once ground. Not to mention, it takes mere seconds to powder your own flax seeds in a spice grinder! If you do opt to purchase flax meal instead, be sure to store the powder in your refrigerator until you are ready to use it. These tiny seeds can be found in bulk bins and prepackaged in the baking aisle of natural food stores.

Graham Cracker Crumbs

When I first went searching for vegan graham crackers, I was appalled by my lack of options. Why every brand in sight needed to include honey was beyond me! So, what is a hungry vegan baker to do in a tight situation like this? Keep on looking, of course. Concealed amongst the rest, and often in natural foods stores, there are a few brands that exclude all animal products. Once you secure your crackers and get them home, you have two options to turn them into crumbs. For a coarse, more varied crumb, toss them into a sturdy plastic bag and just go at it with a rubber mallet! To achieve a fine, even crumb, grind them down in your food processor or spice grinder in batches, and you will have a perfect powder in no time.

Graham Flour

Best known in the form of crackers, graham flour is simply a fancy type of wheat flour. It is made from a process that separates all parts of the wheat kernel itself, and recombines them in different proportions. For reasons beyond my grasp, this particular flour is not sold in all countries. If you are having a hard time getting your hands on some, and don't mind an end product with a slightly different texture, regular old whole wheat flour can be substituted. Of course, you may be able to locate graham flour online and save yourself the worry altogether.

Granulated Sugar

Surprised to see this basic sweetener here? It is true that all sugar (beet or cane) is derived from plant sources and therefore vegan by nature. However, there are some sneaky things going on behind the scenes in big corporations these days. Some cane sugar is filtered using bone char, a very non-vegan process, but it is not specified on any labels. To bypass this problem, many vegans purchase unbleached cane sugar. While it is a suitable substitute, unbleached cane sugar does have a higher molasses content than white sugar, so it tends to produce desserts with a bit more density. Luckily, there are a few caring companies that go through great pains to ensure the purity of their sugar products, such as Florida Crystals and Amalgamated Sugar Company, the suppliers to White Satin, Fred Meyer, Western Family, and Parade. I typically opt for one of these vegan sugar brands to get the best results. As sugar can be a touchy vegan subject, it is best to use your own judgment when considering which brand to purchase.

Matcha/Maccha Powder

Perhaps one of my all-time favorite flavorings, matcha is a very high quality powdered green tea. It is used primarily in Japanese tea ceremonies and can have an intense, bitter taste when used in large amounts. There are many levels of quality, with each step up in grade carrying a higher price tag. Because it can become quite pricey, I would suggest buying a medium grade, which should be readily available at any specialty tea store. When translated directly from Japanese, the spelling is maccha, but the typical English spelling is matcha. Whichever way the package is labeled, you will still find green tea powder within.

Margarine

It is a basic kitchen staple at its core, but good margarine can actually be quite elusive if you do not know what to look for. Some name brands contain whey or other milk-derivatives, while others conceal the elusive, animal-derived Vitamin D3, so be alert when scanning ingredient labels. For ease, I prefer to use stick margarines, such as Earth Balance® or Willow Run®. However, when properly measured, tub margarines should suit most recipes. I always use unsalted margarine unless otherwise noted, but you are welcome to use salted as long as you remove about ¼ teaspoon of salt from the recipe. Overly salted food is one of the first flaws that diners pick up on, so take care with your seasoning!

Puffed Grains

Those crispy rice cereals that have graced breakfast tables for over 50 years are all too familiar, but what about the other puffed grains, such as barley, wheat, or millet? Yes, the exact same process can be used on all of these staples to create light, crunchy cereal grains, each with their own distinctive flavors and shapes. Puffed millet, which I use in the Power Hungry Granola, is perhaps one of the more unusual puffed grains, but it can easily be substituted with puffed rice in an equal proportion should it be difficult to find. I prefer to stick with plain, unaltered grains when making granola. Although the boxed cereals that have sugar added are fine too, just expect a sweeter result. Most health food stores will stock more uncommon varieties in bulk bins, but feel free to experiment with whatever is easiest for you to obtain.

Ricemellow Crème

Remember that old childhood favorite, Marshmallow Fluff®? Well, Ricemellow Crème is its vegan equivalent, void of animal-based gelatins and refined sugars. Light, fluffy, and unlike anything else currently on the market, I have yet to find a suitable vegan alternative for Ricemellow Crème. It can be purchased at most natural food stores, or via online purveyors.

Soy Creamer

Soy creamer is a thicker liquid than regular soymilk, though it is not an equal exchange for dairy-based heavy cream. While it adds richness and moisture to cakes and creamy spreads, soy creamer lacks the proper ratio of proteins necessary to make whipped cream. Rather, it consists primarily of sugars, and consequently boasts a sweeter taste. Soy creamer is available in a number of flavors, all of which may be used for some additional flavoring if desired. In a pinch, regular soymilk or other milk alternative can be substituted, although the end results might not be quite as rich and thick.

Soybean Flour

Ah, what can't this lovely bean do? Going by the name of "Soya" in many parts of the world, soybeans can be dried and finely ground to produce flour. Due to the fat content, soy flour contributes to the density of baked goods and has textural properties similar to those of cocoa powder… but obviously with a much different taste. There are a number of different types of flour made from soybeans, each with varying fat contents. Most of these varietals are only available for commercial use, while one type commonly appears on natural food store shelves. Don't stress, just buy the one that you can find.

Soymilk

Throughout this book, the most common "milk" called for is soymilk, but only because I find that it is widely recognized and the most consistent in flavor of all the current milk alternatives. If you or someone you are baking for is allergic to soy, feel free to substitute almond milk, rice milk, hemp milk, oat milk, or any other milk alternative, to no ill effects. In more delicately flavored dishes, you may be able to taste a faint difference if the substitution is a more distinct milk alternative such as hazelnut, but it should be quite tasty all the same.

Soy Yogurt

Readily available just about everywhere, there are a number of great brands with numerous flavors to choose from. I prefer to purchase single-serving, 6-ounce containers for baking, to avoid leftovers that may go bad while waiting for a new application to come along. Nonetheless, you can certainly save money by purchasing large containers and weighing out the requisite amount.

Tahini

A staple for Middle Eastern cuisine, most regular grocery stores should be able to accommodate your tahini requests. Tahini is a paste very much like peanut butter, but it is made from sesame seeds rather than nuts. If you don't have any on hand and a trip to the market is not in your immediate plans, then any other nut butter will provide exactly the same texture within a recipe, though it will impart a different overall taste.

Textured Vegetable Protein

Typically shortened to the abbreviation of TVP, this is a very concentrated protein, and a byproduct of making soybean oil. It is consequently low in fat, and well known for its appearances in savory dishes as a very convincing meat replacement. Cut into various sizes of chunks, the spongy texture of TVP is especially receptive to other flavors and seasonings. This may sound like a strange ingredient to include within a book about sweet recipes, but bear with me on this one. TVP makes for an excellent addition to granola! Bags or tubs of TVP are available in most health food stores. If you are seriously skeptical and do not want to go through the hassle of finding it, you could possibly leave it out altogether… Just don't tell anyone and I won't either, okay?

Tofu

Yes, I bake with tofu and I don't apologize! It lends fabulous moisture, structure, and even a punch of protein to boot! When I use tofu for baked goods, I always reach for the aseptic, shelf stable packs. Not only do they seem to last forever when unopened, but they also blend down into a perfectly smooth liquid when processed thoroughly. These lovely little boxes are all over the place in natural food stores, so just keep an eye peeled and you should have no problem locating them.

Vegan "Cream Cheese"

Amazingly, many innovative companies now make dairy-free products that will give you the most authentic cream cheese frostings imaginable. These "cheeses" also hold up beautifully in cookie dough and piecrusts, contributing a great tangy flavor and excellent structure. This ingredient is hard to replace, so I suggest that you check out your local mega-mart and natural food grocer, or head online if all else fails.

Vegan "Eggnog"

Made with neither dairy nor eggs, commercially prepared vegan "eggnog" is actually quite delicious, contrary to what thoughts the name may evoke. It is a bit thinner than the traditional egg- and cream- based drink, but this actually makes it even better to bake with, as it doesn't tend to weigh cakes down nearly as much. Due to its seasonality, vegan "eggnog" is only available in the months surrounding Christmas, but during those times you should be able to find it in most mainstream marketplaces. If you cannot wait for the holidays to roll around, then make your own via an online recipe. Simply do a search for "vegan eggnog recipe," to enjoy this indulgence year round.

Vegan "Sour Cream"

Another creative alternative comes to the rescue of vegan bakers everywhere! Vegan "sour cream" provides an amazingly similar, yet dairy-free version of the original tangy spread. In a pinch, I suppose you might be able to get away with using soy yogurt instead, but I really wouldn't recommend it. Vegan "sour cream" is sold in natural food stores and some mainstream grocers. It can often be found neatly tucked in among its dairy-based rivals, or with the other refrigerated dairy alternatives.

Wasabi

Have you ever noticed a big dollop of some green glop in the middle of your veggie sushi that sets your mouth on fire after just one bite? In case you did not know, that unassuming little smear was wasabi. Not typically used in baking but a delight to experiment with, I usually reach for the convenient paste sold in small tubes. However, you can also purchase wasabi in powdered form, and mix it with water until it reaches the proper consistency. Thanks to the growing popularity of Japanese food and world cuisine in general, it should be easy to find wasabi in just about any grocery store.

Whole Wheat Pastry Flour

I just love using whole wheat flour whenever possible, to add in some extra fiber and nutrients, but all too often it can make desserts dense and unpalatable. This is where whole wheat pastry flour steps in! It has a lower gluten content and is therefore less likely to create that tough, heavy texture typically associated with the wholesome grain. White whole wheat flour can also be used for the same applications.

For links to the manufacturers of products I use most, visit: **www.MySweetVegan.com**

For an extensive list of vegan food products and manufacturers, visit: **www.GoDairyFree.org**

Tools of the Trade

Technically speaking, a mixing bowl, big wooden spoon, measuring cups, and a couple of baking tins will allow you to whip up countless fabulous desserts. Nonetheless, a few pieces of supplemental equipment will make your time in the kitchen pass much more quickly and efficiently, improve your end results, and offer the ability to produce some more adventurous recipes. Below is a quick primer on the indispensable gadgets in my kitchen:

Baking Pans/Baking Dishes

There are a wide variety of baking dishes on the market - aluminum, nonstick, glass, silicon, and so on – though any type will generally work, as long as it is the size that the recipe calls for. Just make sure to give your baking pans a little extra attention in the greasing stage if they are not nonstick. Whenever I can, I use nonstick aluminized steel, but bakeware material is greatly a matter of personal preference. For the most part, all of the baking pan shapes and sizes mentioned in this book can be easily found in any good kitchen store, supermarket, or online.

Food Processor

From whipping up the creamiest toppings to preparing homemade nut butter, food processors are one of the best kitchen inventions, in my opinion. For my blending and puréeing needs I use a food processor exclusively, mostly because I cannot afford a blender as well, but I also think that these machines tend to do a more thorough job of breaking down foods. Plus, they typically have a greater capacity than most blenders. Nonetheless, with the exception of grinding nuts into a paste/butter, you can substitute your blender in any recipe that calls for the use of a food processor. As long as your blender can purée, it should work fine. For large recipes, however, you may need to process things in batches if everything doesn't fit in at once.

Piping/Pastry Bags and Tips

The very first time I picked up a piping bag to frost a cupcake, I knew that there was no going back. It just makes for a more professional presentation. If you don't know how to wield a pastry bag or cannot be bothered with the hassle, then there is no need to run out and buy one. However, should you wish to give piping a try, don't skimp on the quality! Piping bags come in heavy-duty, reusable fabric or plastic and disposable varieties, which range in durability. This is one time when I like to use disposable, because piping bags really are a nightmare to clean. Just avoid the cheaper plastic bags, as they are often too thin to stand up to the pressure. As for the tips, you only need one or two big star tips to make a nice "swirly" design. You can also pipe straight out of the bag for a rounded spiral.

Silpats®

I simply adore these flat, nonstick mats and use them at every opportunity. Likened to re-usable parchment paper, silpats cut down on the cost and excess waste of traditional single-use fibers. In terms of performance, silpats also tend to reduce browning, so that it is more difficult (but my no means impossible) to burn cookies when using them. While one should last you several years, it is helpful to have a few on hand. For best care, wash them promptly after each use with mild soap and a soft sponge. Silpats can be located at any good kitchen store.

Spice Grinder

Otherwise known as a coffee grinder, this miniature appliance is so inexpensive and efficient that every home cook should have one! Spice grinders are perfect for quickly grinding nuts, seeds, grains, and of course, spices, into a fine powder. A suitable spice grinder can be found in most supermarkets and kitchen stores.

Springform Pan

Springform pans are a must for creating perfect "cream" and "cheese" cakes. As opposed to standard cake pans, these flexible vessels boast removable sides, which allow softer cakes to remain intact when presented. Springform pans are relatively inexpensive and can be found in most food and kitchen stores. They are easily recognizable by a clamp on one side.

Stand Mixer

While hand mixers get the job done, a good stand mixer will save your arm a tremendous amount of grief. A high-quality stand mixer can cost a pretty penny, but it is usually worth its weight in gold. Powerful and independent, it is easy to multitask while this machine works its magic. If your kitchen space or budget doesn't allow for this luxury, then a hand mixer, or even the vigorous use of a whisk will suit whenever a stand mixer is noted.

SWEET STARTS

Better Banana Nut Muffins

Every good baker should have a reliable banana muffin recipe in his or her repertoire, and this version is my personal favorite. While ordinary recipes merely call for mashed bananas, this one uses rehydrated slices of dried bananas, for a delightfully chewy texture and a truly unique muffin that sets itself apart from the countless lack-luster variations.

Preheat your oven to 375°F (190°C) and lightly grease one dozen muffin tins.

In a small saucepan, combine the dried bananas with about 1 cup of water. Simmer for about 10 minutes to reconstitute them, then remove from the heat and drain off any excess liquid. Once the banana slices are cool enough to handle, roughly chop them into small, bite-sized pieces. Set aside.

Combine the soymilk and vinegar in a large bowl, and let sit for a few minutes before whisking vigorously until frothy. Drizzle in the oil to emulsify, follow with your brown sugar and vanilla, and mix until fully incorporated. Combine the flour, ½ cup oats, baking powder, baking soda, salt, cinnamon, and nutmeg in a separate bowl. Slowly incorporate this dry mixture into the wet, but be careful not to over mix. Fold in the rehydrated bananas, mashed bananas, and pecans. Distribute the batter evenly into your prepared muffin tins.

For the topping, combine the granulated sugar, oats, and cinnamon. Sprinkle it over the raw batter before moving the muffin tins into the oven. Bake for 14 to 18 minutes, until a toothpick inserted into the center of a muffin comes out clean. Let the muffins cool in the tins for at least a few minutes before removing them to a wire rack.

Banana Bread Option: While I love the grab and go convenience of individual muffins, this recipe also makes wonderful banana bread. After preparing the batter, simply pour it into a lightly greased 9 x 5 inch loaf pan. For the topping, combine the granulated sugar, oats, and cinnamon, and sprinkle it over the raw batter before moving the loaf pan into the oven. Bake at 350°F (175°C) for 45 to 55 minutes, until a toothpick inserted into the center of the loaf comes out clean.

Makes 12 Muffins or 1 Medium Loaf

Banana Muffins:
1	Cup Dried Banana Slices
½	Cup Plain Soymilk
½	Teaspoon Apple Cider Vinegar
¼	Cup Canola or Vegetable Oil
¼	Cup Dark Brown Sugar
½	Teaspoon Vanilla Extract
1	Cup All-Purpose Flour
½	Cup Rolled Oats
1	Teaspoon Baking Powder
½	Teaspoon Baking Soda
¼	Teaspoon Salt
½	Teaspoon Ground Cinnamon
1	Dash of Ground Nutmeg
2	Large Bananas, Mashed
½	Cup Chopped Pecans

Oat Topping:
2	Tablespoons Granulated Sugar
2	Tablespoons Rolled Oats
¼	Teaspoon Ground Cinnamon

Better Banana Nut Muffins

Chocolate-Glazed Peanut Butter Scones

In my book, peanut butter is perhaps the perfect spread. It comes in countless varieties to suit every taste, and it is an excellent addition to baked goods! In these scones, peanut butter is used not only as a flavorful bonus, but also as a key to the structure. It actually takes the place of some of the margarine, for a healthier treat. Naturally, I used this logic to help justify the chocolate peanut butter glaze drizzled over the top. Nice to your body and just a little bit naughty, these may be the ultimate breakfast baked-good!

Peanut Butter Scones:

1½	Cups All-Purpose Flour
2	Tablespoons Granulated Sugar
2	Teaspoons Baking Powder
¼	Teaspoon Salt
2	Tablespoons Margarine
¼	Cup Crunchy Peanut Butter
1	Teaspoon Vanilla Extract
½	Cup Plain Soymilk

Chocolate Peanut Butter Glaze:

⅓	Cup Confectioner's Sugar
½	Tablespoon Dutch Process Cocoa Powder
1	Tablespoon Creamy Peanut Butter
1	Tablespoon Plain Soymilk

Preheat your oven to 400°F (205°C) and line a baking sheet with a silpat or parchment paper.

[This step may be done in a food processor] In a medium bowl, combine the flour, sugar, baking powder, and salt. Cut the margarine into small pieces, and use a fork or a pastry cutter to press both the margarine and the crunchy peanut butter into the flour mixture. Continue cutting the fats in until the mixture resembles large, coarse crumbs, at which point you can stir in the vanilla. Slowly drizzle in the soymilk one tablespoon at a time, stirring just until the dough starts to come together into a ball. Try not to overwork the dough any more than necessary.

Drop all of the dough onto your silpat and shape it into a rough circle. This is rather sticky dough, but work with it gently and it should cooperate. Cut this circle into 4 quarters, each looking somewhat triangular, and separate them on the baking sheet so that each has room to cook. Bake for 15 to 20 minutes, until they turn a light golden brown. Cool your scones on the baking sheet for at least 5 minutes.

For the glaze, combine the confectioner's sugar, cocoa, peanut butter, and soymilk together in a small bowl. Mix thoroughly until smooth, and drizzle over the cooled scones.

Makes 4 Scones

Chocolate-Glazed Peanut Butter Scones

Dried Fruit Focaccia

I know, I know, focaccia is supposed to be savory bread containing tomatoes, herbs, and what have you; but why let the traditional definition limit your creativity? Prepared with sweet dried fruits, this simple yet satisfying yeast bread is a wonderful treat to help jump start your day. Of course, any combination of dried fruit add-ins should work well, so use your favorites if you aren't keen on my recommendations!

3	Cups Water (Reserve 1 Cup After Soaking)
1	Cup Dried Cranberries
1	Cup Raisins
1	Cup Dried, Chopped Apricots
1	Cup Orange Juice
¼	Cup Olive Oil
1	Packet Active Dry Yeast
5–6	Cups All-Purpose Flour
¾	Cup Granulated Sugar, Divided
1	Teaspoon Salt

Bring the water to a boil in a large pot and turn off the heat. Add in the dried fruit and let it soak for about 15 minutes to rehydrate. Drain the fruit, but save 1 cup of the liquid. In a medium bowl, mix the reserved soaking liquid with the orange juice, oil, and yeast. Set aside.

Into a large bowl, toss the rehydrated fruit along with 2 cups of flour, ½ cup of sugar, and the salt. Add in about half of your liquid ingredients, and mix thoroughly until you achieve a smooth dough. Add in another 2 cups of flour along with the remainder of the liquid, and mix again. You don't want the dough to be too sticky, so you may need to introduce anywhere from 1 to 2 more cups of flour, depending on the moisture content of your dough. At this point, you may need to work the dough with either a dough hook installed in your stand mixer or your hands. When it is finished combining, you should have a cohesive ball of dough that can be easily handled. Continue to mix it with the dough hook, or knead vigorously by hand on a lightly floured surface, for about 5 to 10 minutes, until the dough becomes glutinous and elastic.

Thoroughly grease a 12 x 17 inch jellyroll pan and spread the dough on top. Use your fingers to poke the dough down at random, and let the pan sit in a warm place to rise for about an hour. When it appears to have doubled in volume, sprinkle the dough evenly with the remaining ¼ cup of sugar, and bake in a 400°F (205°C) oven for 25 to 30 minutes. When it is done, the bread should have a solid crust that is a deep golden brown. Let cool and slice into 3 x 4 inch pieces.

Enjoy this stand-alone breakfast bread as is, or add even more fruit flavor with your favorite jam.

Makes 16 Servings

Dried Fruit Focaccia

Golden Glazed Donuts

Remember those crispy, creamy donuts of unsavory origin, oozing with cholesterol and animal fat? Well, these are not a carbon copy to say the least, heavens no... they are much better! Instead of just melting away to coat your tongue in sugary lard, these donuts actually offer some substance. Certainly these are still a far cry from health food, but they are donuts after all!

Donuts:
- 1 Packet Active Dry Yeast
- 2 Tablespoons Warm Water
- 3 Tablespoons Vegetable Shortening
- ¼ Cup Granulated Sugar
- 1 Tablespoon Flax Seeds
- ¾ Cup Plain Soymilk
- 1 Teaspoon Apple Cider Vinegar
- ½ Teaspoon Vanilla Extract
- ½ Teaspoon Salt
- 2½ Cups All-Purpose Flour
- 1 Quart Canola or Vegetable Oil for Frying

Glaze:
- 3 Tablespoons Margarine
- 1 Cup Confectioner's Sugar
- 1 Teaspoon Vanilla Extract
- 1 Tablespoon Water

Sprinkle the yeast over the warm water in a small dish, and let sit for 5 minutes, until it wakes up and becomes a bit frothy. Meanwhile, in your stand mixer, cream the shortening and sugar together and beat until fluffy. Grind the flax seeds into a fine powder using a spice grinder, and add it into the mixer along with the soymilk, vinegar, vanilla, and salt. Incorporate the watery yeast. Add in 2 cups of flour, letting the mixer run until it is fully mixed in. Add in the remaining ½ cup of flour, and continue mixing to combine. Replace the beaters with a dough hook if you have one, and agitate the dough on a medium speed for about 5 minutes; or move the dough out onto a lightly floured surface and knead it by hand. If using a stand mixer, turn the dough out onto a lightly floured surface once the 5 minutes are up, and knead it a few times by hand, so that it feels smooth and elastic. Move the dough into a lightly greased bowl, cover, and place in a warm location to allow it to rise. Wait for the dough to double in volume before proceeding, approximately 1 hour.

On a lightly floured surface, turn the dough out of the bowl and gently roll it out to about ½ inch thick. Use a donut cutter, or one large and one small circular cookie cutter, lightly dipped in flour to create each shape. Move the raw donuts onto a greased baking sheet. Cut any remaining dough into small circles to make donut holes, and move these onto the baking sheet. Cover the cut dough shapes loosely with a towel, and let them rise for another hour or so, until they double in size.

Once the dough is ready, begin heating the oil in a deep fryer or large skillet. While the oil is heating, prepare the glaze. Over medium-low heat, melt the margarine and then whisk in the sugar, vanilla, and water until the glaze is completely smooth. Pour the glaze into a shallow dish that is wide enough to accommodate your donuts. Set aside. Don't worry if the glaze begins to solidify while you are frying, the heat from the donuts should melt it once more.

The oil should be at 350°F (175°C) when you are ready to start frying. First and foremost, be very careful! Cooking only one or two donuts at a time, carefully slide the raw dough into the oil using a wide slotted spatula. Fry them for about 2 minutes per side, until deeply golden brown. Remove the cooked donuts using the same spatula, briefly pat any excess oil off using a paper towel, and dip them in your glaze while still warm. Repeat this process for the donut holes and remaining scraps of dough. Let the donuts sit on a cooling rack for at least 10 minutes before consuming, as they will be quite hot.

Makes 6 Full-Sized Donuts plus 6 or more Donut Holes

Golden Glazed Donuts

Graham Flour Fig Scones

Simple to make yet so unique in both flavor and texture, these scones belong in a category all their own. As long as you have these wholesome biscuits on hand, it will be easy to start every day off on the right foot. Try them lightly toasted with a pat of margarine slowly melting over the top for a delicious wake-up call.

Though it will create a different product, you can substitute more whole wheat pastry flour if graham flour is not within your grasp.

Preheat your oven to 375°F (190°C) and line a baking sheet with a silpat or parchment paper.

In a medium bowl, combine the flours, sugar, baking powder, and salt. Cut the margarine into small pieces, and use your fingers or a pastry cutter to press it into the flour mixture. Continue coating as many grains as possible until you create a coarse, sandy consistency. Stir in the figs and vanilla. Add the soy creamer, one tablespoon at a time, until the mixture just comes together as cohesive dough. The amount depends on your humidity level, so don't be afraid to use either more or less than suggested if it seems appropriate.

Turn the dough out of the bowl, and firmly press it into a circle that is about one inch tall. Cut your circle into even quarters and carefully move the divided dough onto your prepared baking sheet. Bake for 14 to 16 minutes, until the scones just begin to brown around the edges. Let cool on the sheet, and serve with a dollop of fruit preserves or margarine.

Makes 4 Scones

1	Cup Graham Flour
½	Cup Whole Wheat Pastry Flour
⅓	Cup Granulated Sugar
2	Teaspoons Baking Powder
¼	Teaspoon Salt
¼	Cup Margarine
¾	Cups Chopped Dried Figs
1	Teaspoon Vanilla Extract
4–6	Tablespoons Plain Soy Creamer

Graham Flour Fig Scones

Oatmeal Raisin Rolls

¾	Cup Plain Soymilk
1	Packet Active Dry Yeast
¼	Cup Margarine
¼	Cup Granulated Sugar
1	Teaspoon Vanilla Extract
1	Tablespoon Baking Powder
½	Teaspoon Salt
1¼	Cups Whole Wheat Pastry Flour
1¼	Cups Rolled Oats
1	Cup All-Purpose Flour
½	Cup Dark Brown Sugar
¼	Cup Raisins

Cinnamon buns are a delight in the morning, unless of course you are the baker who had to wake up extra early to make them. You could choose the traditional route, agonizing over long waiting periods while the dough rises... but why not make a different sort of swirled bun that isn't nearly so fussy? These rolls come together very quickly and are much heartier than the original pastry, so you can still feel virtuous for eating a good breakfast!

Preheat your oven to 400°F (205°C) and line a baking sheet with a silpat or parchment paper.

Heat the soymilk in a microwave-safe dish for 30 to 60 seconds, or until it is just warmed through. Add the yeast and let sit until it becomes frothy, about 5 minutes. Meanwhile, in a separate bowl, cream the margarine, sugar, and vanilla together. Add in the baking powder, salt, whole wheat flour, and oats, mixing thoroughly to combine. The yeast should have become visibly active by now, so pour the yeast and soymilk into the batter, and mix thoroughly. Finally, add the all-purpose flour, and stir well, so that everything is completely combined.

Turn the dough out onto a generously floured surface and knead it briefly for up to 5 minutes. Press the dough out manually to form a nice even rectangle of about ¼ inch thickness. Exact measurements aren't all that important, but keep in mind that a longer, thinner shape will produce more rolls that are smaller, while a shorter, wider shape will produce fewer rolls that are larger and have more layers. Regardless of what you ultimately end up with, sprinkle the brown sugar evenly over the top, leaving about 1 inch on one of the long sides clear. Sprinkle the raisins over the brown sugar, and press it all gently into the surface of the dough. Starting at the long side where the sugar goes all the way to the edge, roll the dough carefully without stretching or pulling it. When you get to the edge, very lightly moisten the clean edge of dough with water so that it sticks to the side. Lay the dough seam-side down on the counter, and gently cut 1-inch pieces with a very sharp knife. Place each roll on your prepared baking sheet, with one of the cut sides down, and bake for 15 to 20 minutes, until they just begin to turn golden brown.

Enjoy these rolls as a breakfast sweet, or top them with a sugary icing for a decadent dessert.

Makes 12 to 15 Rolls

Oatmeal Raisin Rolls

Power Hungry Granola

On typical school days, my go-to breakfast is almost always some sort of granola. Instant, easy to eat, and delicious, I could probably live on nothing but cereals for days on end. Unfortunately, many commercial granolas are pumped full of sugars and extra oils to make them more like candy than grains! After experiencing devastating crashes from sugar rushes that left me high and dry halfway through my 2nd class of the day, I decided that I would just have to make my own. Full of whole grains, protein, good fats and just enough sweetness to entice the taste buds, this concoction put an end to my midday slumps.

Really, nothing could be easier than making granola. Double or even triple this recipe, and you will have more than enough for the week ahead.

Preheat your oven to 300°F (150°C) and lightly grease a jellyroll pan, or any other large dish with shallow sides.

With a large spatula, stir together the TVP, oats, millet, and cinnamon in a large bowl. In a separate bowl, combine the sugar and all of the liquid ingredients (vanilla through oil). Pour the liquid over the dry, folding it together until all of the cereal is completely moistened. Spread as flat a layer as possible into your prepared pan or dish. Bake for 30 to 35 minutes, stirring at 10-minute intervals so that your granola doesn't burn. Let it cool completely on the sheet.

Once cool, stir in the cranberries and almonds, and serve with your favorite milk alternative. Store any leftover granola in an airtight container.

Makes 4 to 6 Servings

1	Cup Textured Vegetable Protein (TVP)
1	Cup Rolled Oats
3	Cups Puffed Millet
2	Teaspoons Ground Cinnamon
1/3	Cup Dark Brown Sugar
1/2	Teaspoon Vanilla Extract
1/4	Cup Maple Syrup
1/3	Cup Apple Juice
1	Tablespoon Canola or Vegetable Oil
2/3	Cup Dried Cranberries
1/2	Cup Sliced Almonds

Power Hungry Granola

Strawberry Love Muffins

They say that the quickest way to a person's heart is through their stomach. Thus, it seems only logical that when Valentine's Day rolls around, something edible must take center stage. While chocolate and candies are obvious considerations, try this equally romantic treat for those who prefer a sweet that doesn't carry the guilt of an over-the-top indulgence. Of course, regularly shaped muffins that don't take the form of hearts work just as well if you lack the necessary equipment. Whatever vessel ends up becoming a home to your blushing batter, these muffins are guaranteed to elicit gratitude and delight.

Preheat your oven to 375°F (190°C) and grease one dozen muffin tins.

Begin by mixing together your dry ingredients (flour through salt) in a large bowl. Gently stir in the soymilk, oil, and vanilla but be careful not to over mix, a few lumps are okay! Fold in the thawed strawberries and pour the batter into your prepared muffin tins, ¾ of the way to the top. Slide your filled tins into the oven and bake for 15 to 20 minutes, until a toothpick inserted into the center of a muffin comes out clean.

Let the muffins sit for at least 10 minutes before removing them from the pan. Enjoy with someone you love.

Makes 12 Muffins

1½	Cups All-Purpose Flour
½	Cup Granulated Sugar
1	Teaspoon Baking Powder
1	Teaspoon Baking Soda
¼	Teaspoon Salt
¾	Cup Plain Soymilk
⅓	Cup Canola or Vegetable Oil
1	Teaspoon Vanilla Extract
1	Cup Frozen Strawberries, Thawed and Sliced

Sweet & Simple French Toast

When I first attempted French toast it was still very early in my "career" as a vegan. Because I had yet to really move into my element in the kitchen, my whole family remained skeptical of what could be done without milk or eggs. Even my mom, the eternal optimist, was not exactly convinced that French toast without the usual animal products could be the least bit palatable. Still, I persevered and came up with this creation to share with her. All it took was one mouthful of this delicious dish for my mother to start thinking about veganism in an entirely different way.

4	Slices Whole Wheat Bread
2	Tablespoons Whole Wheat Flour
1	Teaspoon Nutritional Yeast
2	Tablespoons Dark Brown Sugar
¼	Teaspoon Salt
½	Teaspoon Ground Cinnamon
1	Pinch Ground Nutmeg
1	Cup Plain Soymilk

Begin by lightly toasting your bread, allowing it to become a bit firmer, and more receptive to the extra moisture that you will be adding.

Combine the dry ingredients in a shallow pan and make sure that they are evenly distributed. Stir in the soymilk and allow it to sit for a minute or two. Whisk again before using, to ensure that no lumps are left behind. Soak your first two pieces of toast in this wet mixture while heating up a skillet on the stove. Grease the pan lightly with a nonstick spray, or a small pat of margarine, if desired.

Flip your toast over and let the wet mixture absorb into the other side for another minute or two. Once they appear to be fully saturated, carefully lift the slices out with a large spatula and place them into the hot skillet. On medium high heat, fry them for approximately 3 to 5 minutes per side. Everyone's stove is different, so keep a close eye on your toast.

Once nicely browned and crisp on the outside, transfer the toast to a plate, and repeat the process with the two remaining bread slices. Serve with maple syrup, fruit spread, or powdered sugar as you see fit.

Makes 4 Slices

Sweet & Simple French Toast

Zesty Cranberry Crumb Muffins

Streusel just makes everything better, doesn't it? While these muffins are incredibly good on their own, the crumbly topping bumps them up that extra notch to irresistible. Tangy, tart, and sweet all at the same time, the flavors and textures seem to work in perfect harmony. This treat is perfectly acceptable as a breakfast, but delicious as an afternoon snack as well.

Preheat your oven to 375°F (190°C) and lightly grease one dozen muffin tins.

Combine the cranberries and orange juice in a saucepan and simmer over medium-low heat for about 10 minutes, until the fruit has absorbed all of the liquid. Remove from the heat and let cool.

Combine the soymilk and vinegar in a large bowl, and let sit for a few minutes before whisking vigorously until frothy. Incorporate the oil into the soymilk mixture and beat until fully emulsified. Add the sugar, and mix well. Add in the flours, baking powder, baking soda, and applesauce, being careful not to over mix. Gently fold in the rehydrated cranberries and zest. Spoon the batter into your prepared muffin tins.

For the crumb topping, combine the margarine, flour, and sugar with a pastry cutter or fork, until it resembles coarse crumbs. Sprinkle evenly over each mound of raw batter. Bake for 14 to 18 minutes, until a toothpick inserted into the center of a muffin comes out clean. Let the muffins sit for at least 10 minutes before removing them from the pan.

Makes 12 Muffins

Cranberry Muffins:

¾	Cup Dried Cranberries
¾	Cup Orange Juice
½	Cup Plain Soymilk
1	Teaspoon Apple Cider Vinegar
⅓	Cup Canola or Vegetable Oil
⅔	Cup Granulated Sugar
1	Cup All-Purpose Flour
½	Cup Whole Wheat Pastry Flour
1½	Teaspoons Baking Powder
½	Teaspoon Baking Soda
3	Tablespoons Unsweetened Applesauce
2	Tablespoons Orange Zest

Crumb Topping:

3	Tablespoons Margarine
⅓	Cup All-Purpose Flour
⅓	Cup Granulated Sugar

Zesty Cranberry Crumb Muffins

COOKIES & BARS

Almond Avalanche Bars

Almonds are all the rage for health nuts and foodies alike, due to their high levels of antioxidants, unsaturated fats, and of course, delicious taste. If you happen to be one of those almond fanatics who simply can't get enough, then this bar was made for you. Practically bursting with nutty goodness in each layer, just one small bar is a seriously satisfying snack. In fact, a larger helping could possibly be considered a heart-healthy breakfast!

Preheat your oven to 350°F (175°C) and grease a 9 x 13 inch baking pan.

In a medium bowl, cream together the margarine and sugar until homogeneous. Slowly incorporate the almond meal, followed by the salt. Transfer the mixture into your prepared baking pan and pat the dough into the bottom, keeping it as even as possible. Bake for 15 to 18 minutes, until firm and lightly browned. Let cool, but leave the oven on.

For the topping, dump all of the almond butter into your mixer and add the corn syrup, sugar, and vanilla. Blend until smooth and fully combined. Fold in the chocolate chips, if desired. Drop this mixture evenly over your crust, pressing if necessary to form an even layer. Sprinkle the sliced almonds over the top, and bake for about 15 more minutes. You are not looking for a dry exterior, so it is okay if the bars look moist or under-baked. A raw cookie dough appearance is what you are going for.

Let cool COMPLETELY before cutting into bars. By completely, I don't mean cool to the touch. The bars must be cool enough for the chocolate chips to re-solidify. If you are not patient, you may end up with a fudgy almond mess!

Makes 24 to 36 Bars

Almond Crust:
½	Cup Margarine
½	Cup Dark Brown Sugar
1⅓	Cups Almond Meal
½	Teaspoon Salt

Almond Topping:
16	Ounces Almond Butter
1	Cup Light Corn Syrup
½	Cup Granulated Sugar
2	Teaspoons Vanilla Extract
1	Cup Dark or Semi-Sweet Chocolate Chips (Optional)
1	Cup Sliced Almonds

Almond Avalanche Bars

Apricot Biscotti

For such a humble name, these cafe-inspired treats boast an impressive array of complex flavors. While they are made with vastly different ingredients and techniques than your typical biscotti, the careful attention to each individual component really does produce superior results. These biscotti are suitable for the gluten intolerant, yet the overall taste is so spot-on that they would be right at home in any coffee house. Lightly drizzled with a sugary glaze, a quick dip in your coffee or tea will leave the beverage with an extra hint of sweetness to linger long after the cookie is gone.

Preheat your oven to 325°F (160°C) and lightly grease two 9 x 5 inch loaf pans.

In a small saucepan over medium heat, cover the chopped apricots with water and bring to a boil. Reduce the heat and simmer for about 15 minutes, until most of the water has been absorbed. Drain any excess liquid, and set the apricots aside to cool.

If using whole almonds, place them in your food processor or blender, and grind them down into as fine a powder as you can manage without allowing a paste to form. In a medium bowl, combine your freshly processed or prepackaged almond meal with the cornmeal and cornstarch, stirring until blended. Mix in the granulated sugar and baking soda.

In a separate large bowl, stir together the soy yogurt, maple syrup, oil, and vanilla until fully emulsified. Sift the dry ingredients into this bowl slowly, stirring until everything is completely combined with no lumps. You don't need to worry about over mixing because there is no gluten involved! Finally, fold in the apricots that you had previously set aside.

Divide the dough evenly between the two loaf pans and pat it into the bottom, pressing the dough as smoothly as possible. Bake for 30 to 35 minutes, until lightly browned on the outside and cooked through the center. Let the biscotti loaves sit inside the pans for 5 minutes before turning them out onto a wire rack, where they should sit for an additional 15 minutes.

Raise the oven temperature to 350°F (175°C) and line a baking sheet with a silpat or parchment paper. Slice the biscotti loaves into individual cookies, about ½ inch thick each. Lay the cookies with one of the cut sides down on the prepared baking sheet, and bake for 15 minutes. Flip the biscotti over onto their other cut side, and bake for another 15 minutes. Cool the biscotti completely on a wire rack.

To finish them off, simply melt the margarine and mix in the confectioner's sugar and vanilla until smooth. Drizzle this glaze over the biscotti. Alternately, you could dip the biscotti halfway into the icing for a sweeter finish.

Makes Approximately 24 Biscotti

Biscotti:

1	Cup Dried Apricots, Chopped
1	Cup Whole Dry Roasted, Unsalted Almonds or 1 Scant Cup Almond Meal
1	Cup Cornmeal
1	Cup Cornstarch
½	Cup Granulated Sugar
½	Teaspoon Baking Soda
6	Ounces Vanilla Soy Yogurt
¼	Cup Maple Syrup
1	Tablespoon Canola or Vegetable Oil
1	Teaspoon Vanilla Extract

Glaze:

1	Tablespoon Margarine
½	Cup Confectioner's Sugar
½	Teaspoon Vanilla Extract

Apricot Biscotti

Black & Whites

As a young child, my parents often took my sister and me into New York City, to see the sights and experience a slice of the life that they once lived. This was always a fantastic treat, but my favorite part was our ritual of stopping at a bakery just before boarding the train back home, and picking up a black and white cookie. Every time I chose that same cookie, yet the repetition never wore on my taste buds. Though the egg-based originals from New York are no longer an option, this updated classic tastes as authentic as anything you could find in or outside of the city.

Cookie Base:

2	Cups All-Purpose Flour
1	Teaspoon Baking Powder
½	Teaspoon Baking Soda
¼	Teaspoon Salt
½	Cup Margarine
1	Cup Granulated Sugar
1	Tablespoon Flax Seeds
2	Tablespoons Water
2	Teaspoons Vanilla Extract
½	Cup Vegan "Sour Cream"

Vanilla Icing:

2	Cups Confectioner's Sugar
3	Tablespoons Plain Soy Creamer
¼	Teaspoon Vanilla Extract

Chocolate Icing:

3	Ounces Dark Chocolate, Roughly Chopped
¼	Cup Plain Soy Creamer
1	Tablespoon Light Corn Syrup
1	Cup Confectioner's Sugar

Preheat your oven to 350°F (175°C) and line two baking sheets with silpats or parchment paper.

Sift together the flour, baking powder, baking soda and salt in a medium bowl and set aside. In your stand mixer, cream the margarine and granulated sugar until soft and fully combined. Grind the flax seeds into a powder with a spice grinder, and whiz them together with the water. Add the flax seed mixture to your mixer. Incorporate the vanilla and "sour cream," scraping down the sides of the bowl as necessary to achieve a completely smooth mixture. Slowly add in the flour mixture, stirring just enough to combine without any lumps remaining.

Onto the prepared baking sheets, drop about ¼ cup of dough for each cookie, leaving plenty of room for them to spread, roughly three inches between each. Lightly moisten your hands to prevent sticking and gently pat the dough mounds into approximately 2½ inch disks. Bake for 14 to 17 minutes, until they just begin to turn slightly golden in color. Let the cookies rest on the baking sheet for 2 additional minutes, and then transfer them to a wire rack to cool completely.

For the vanilla icing, whisk together 1 cup of the confectioner's sugar in a small bowl with the soy creamer and vanilla, ensuring that you have a completely smooth mixture. Add in the remaining 1 cup of sugar and combine. Even though it may seem too dry at first, continue stirring and it will soon reveal itself as a nice, thick icing. Set aside.

For the chocolate icing, place the chocolate, soy creamer, and corn syrup in a microwave-safe bowl and heat for 30 to 60 seconds, just until the chocolate begins to melt. Stir rapidly and thoroughly to combine all of the ingredients, until the chocolate is completely smooth. Set aside to cool while you continue to work. Starting with the vanilla icing, use a spatula to spread the white glaze on half of each cookie. Let the glaze set for at least 10 minutes.

Returning to your chocolate icing, add in the 1 cup of confectioner's sugar and stir until completely smooth. Spread on the other half of each cookie. Let the cookies sit until the glaze has fully set up.

Makes 12 Large Cookies

Black & Whites

Black Bottom Blondies

Chocolate or vanilla? Brownies or blondies? There really is no need to agonize over these tough choices when you can have them all in one bar! Not only is this a perfect combo bar for the indecisive eater, but the prolific baker as well, tackling two types of sweets at once without even dirtying an extra pan! Both your taste buds and busy schedule will certainly be pleased with the convenience of this delicious bar that could hardly be considered a compromise.

½	Cup Margarine
6	Ounces Vanilla Soy Yogurt
½	Cup Dark Brown Sugar
¾	Cup Granulated Sugar
½	Cup Plain Soymilk
1	Tablespoon Vanilla Extract
⅛	Teaspoon Salt
1¾	Cups All-Purpose Flour
⅓	Cup Dutch Process Cocoa Powder
¼	Cup Semi-Sweet Chocolate Chips

Preheat your oven to 350°F (175°C) and grease an 8 x 8 inch square baking pan.

Melt your margarine and let cool for a minute or two before pouring it into a stand mixer and stirring in the soy yogurt. Add in both sugars and mix thoroughly. Blend in the soymilk, then the vanilla extract, followed by a healthy pinch of salt. Slowly sprinkle in the flour, pausing occasionally to let the mixer process everything together.

Once the batter is more or less homogeneous, remove 1 cup and pour it into a separate bowl. Stir the cocoa and chocolate chips into this portion, and smooth it evenly into the bottom of your prepared dish. It will be very thick, so you may need to coerce it into position. Pour the remaining batter, waiting inside the mixer, over this base and spread evenly. Bake for 28 to 35 minutes, until the sides pull away from the pan and the top turns golden brown. Let cool completely before cutting.

Makes 9 to 12 Bars

Black Bottom Blondies

Butterscotch Blondies

This particular childhood favorite turned out to be one of the most difficult recipes for me to master. Really, it should have been a breeze to figure out this seemingly foolproof idea, and yet my first trial pan of raw batter literally exploded all over the oven. I wish I were exaggerating, but in all honesty, drippy streaks of sugar and margarine plastered the glass window from which I watched in horror. Thankfully, though it took a while to perfect my approach, the following 5 or 6 attempts only resulted in a trash can full of unsatisfactory baked goods rather than more kitchen disasters. Now, I am happy to share my easy method for creating this sweet treat that I remember fondly from my pre-vegan days. It doesn't require you to blow anything up, either.

¼	Cup Margarine
1½	Cups Dark Brown Sugar
1½	Teaspoons Vanilla Extract
6	Ounces Vanilla Soy Yogurt
⅓	Cup Plain Soy Creamer
2	Cups All-Purpose Flour
2	Teaspoons Baking Powder

Preheat your oven to 350°F (175°C) and lightly grease an 8 x 8 inch square baking pan.

Melt the margarine and pour it over the brown sugar in a medium bowl, stirring to coat. Add the vanilla, soy yogurt, and soy creamer, and stir until homogeneous. Slowly incorporate the flour along with the baking powder, stirring just enough to arrive at a smooth mixture. Pour the batter into your prepared pan. Bake for 25 to 30 minutes, until the sides just begin to pull away from the pan and the top is fairly firm. The blondies may still be slightly gooey on the inside, but they will continue to cook once removed from the oven. Besides, they are "fudgy" bars, so you don't want them to dry out! Wait for the blondies to cool completely before cutting.

Makes 9 to 12 Bars

Butterscotch Blondies

"Cheese" Cake Thumbprint Cookies

Even better than individual cheesecakes, these are such small indulgences that you need not feel the least bit guilty. In fact, you do not even need to pull up a seat or grab a fork to dig in! Perfect on the go or with a tall cup of coffee, these no-fuss sweets are much easier to make, bring to events, and eat after a filling meal than a standard cheesecake. If you would like to add another flavor to the party, go ahead and top them with fruit preserves for the authentic yet effortless taste of a fruit-topped cheesecake.

The "graham" flavor is important in this cookie. If you are unable to find graham flour, grind some vegan graham crackers into a very fine powder for a suitable substitute.

To prepare the filling, begin by stirring the "cream cheese" with a spatula in a medium bowl to soften it a bit. Add in the sugar and salt, and cream thoroughly. Pour in the soy creamer and vanilla, mixing until you have a completely homogeneous mixture. Stirring rapidly, sprinkle in the arrowroot, mixing until smooth and creamy once more. Refrigerate this mixture for at least 30 minutes.

While the filling chills, preheat your oven to 350°F (175°C) and line two baking sheets with silpats or parchment paper.

For the cookie part, use your stand mixer to cream the margarine and sugar together. Grind the flax seeds into a powder with a spice grinder, and whiz them together with the water. Add the flax mixture to your stand mixer along with the oil, and combine well. Add in the graham flour first, making sure it is fully incorporated before following it with the all-purpose flour. Once the second flour enters the mixer, be careful to mix it for just long enough to bring the dough together and not a minute longer, lest you get a tougher cookie.

Scoop out balls of dough that are about an inch or so in diameter, and roll them into fairly smooth spheres with you hands. Drop the spheres onto your prepared baking sheets, and use either your fingers or the handle of a wooden spoon to make an indentation into the center of each. Bake the cookies for 10 minutes before checking on their progress. If your indentations are on the shallow side, you should take this opportunity to press the centers back in and reshape any other abnormalities. Bake for another 7 to 9 minutes, until they begin to take on a bit of color.

Remove the cookies from the oven in order to fill them with the mixture that has been chilling in your refrigerator. Spoon about 2 to 3 teaspoons of filling into the center of each cookie, and return them once more to the oven to bake for an additional 8 minutes or so. The filling will begin to puff up a bit and solidify when they are done. Let the cookies sit for 2 minutes on the sheet before moving them to a wire rack to finish cooling.

Makes Approximately 30 Cookies

"Cheese" Filling:

4	Ounces Vegan "Cream Cheese"
¼	Cup Granulated Sugar
⅛	Teaspoon Salt
1	Tablespoon Plain Soy Creamer
¼	Teaspoon Vanilla Extract
1	Teaspoon Arrowroot Powder

Cookie:

½	Cup Margarine
¼	Cup Granulated Sugar
1	Tablespoon Flax Seeds
2	Tablespoons Water
2	Tablespoons Canola or Vegetable Oil
1	Cup Graham Flour
1	Cup All-Purpose Flour

"Cheese" Cake Thumbprint Cookies

Coffee Break Shortbread

Long school days followed by hours of homework have taught me at least one important lesson: Never plan an all-nighter without arming yourself with plenty of coffee! Even better yet, grab a stack of cookies with all of the delicious flavors and energizing caffeine inside! Bake up a big batch of these shortbread cookies for your study group, and everyone will surely thank you.

½	Cup Confectioner's Sugar
½	Cup Margarine
1	Tablespoon Instant Coffee Powder
1	Teaspoon Vanilla Extract
1	Cup All-Purpose Flour
¼	Teaspoon Salt

Cream together the sugar and margarine in your stand mixer, followed by the instant coffee and vanilla extract. Slowly mix in the flour and salt until it starts to become incorporated. You may need to run your mixer for a minute and rest the dough, and then mix again to create smooth results. The dough will start off looking very crumbly and dry, but resist the urge to add liquid; it will come together if you give it time! Once you have a solid, cohesive ball of dough, refrigerate it for at least an hour.

Once you pull the dough from the refrigerator, preheat your oven to 325°F (160°C) and line two baking sheets with silpats or parchment paper.

Roll out the dough using a rolling pin lightly coated in confectioner's sugar to prevent sticking; ⅛ inch in thickness is ideal. Cut the dough into desired shapes using cookie cutters, and move the cookies onto your prepared baking sheets. Baking time can vary greatly, from 14 minutes and up depending on the size of your shapes. Don't wait for them brown very much, but they should be somewhat firm to the touch when done. Remove the cookies from the baking sheet to cool.

Makes 12 to 24 Cookies

Coffee Break Shortbread

Crumb-Topped Brownies

Whenever I baked my chocolate crumb cupcakes, everyone would rave about the sweet, cocoa crumb topping. Trying to work out a new and improved recipe for my standard brownies, it was a moment of pure inspiration when I considered combining the best part of those two sweets into one amazing chocolate experience. I am not so conceited as to declare that these are the best brownies ever... but I will let you come to that conclusion for yourself.

Preheat your oven to 350°F (175°C) and grease an 8 x 8 inch square baking pan.

To make the topping, combine the granulated sugar, cocoa, and flour in a small bowl. Add in the oil, and stir well so that everything is incorporated. Add in the confectioner's sugar, taking care to coat as much of the mixture as possible, while breaking up the topping into small and medium sized crumbs. Set aside.

For the main batter, melt your margarine and let it cool down a bit before using. In a stand mixer, combine the soy yogurt and both sugars, followed by the margarine. Stir thoroughly, and then pour in the soy creamer. The coffee powder and vanilla can be mixed in at this point as well. Add in the flour, cocoa, and salt. Pause occasionally to allow the mixer to catch up to your demands, but rest assured that it will all come together in due time. Fold in the chips by hand, and smooth the batter into your prepared pan.

Sprinkle your crumb topping over the raw batter and bake for 25 to 28 minutes, until the sides pull away from the pan slightly. Allow the brownies to cool completely before cutting.

Makes 9 to 12 Brownies

Crumb Topping:

¼	Cup Granulated Sugar
¼	Cup Dutch Process Cocoa Powder
2	Tablespoons All-Purpose Flour
2	Tablespoons Canola or Vegetable Oil
2	Tablespoons Confectioner's Sugar

Brownies:

¼	Cup Margarine
6	Ounces Black Cherry Soy Yogurt
¼	Cup Dark Brown Sugar
½	Cup Granulated Sugar
⅓	Cup Plain Soy Creamer
½	Teaspoon Instant Coffee Powder
1	Teaspoon Vanilla Extract
¾	Cup All-Purpose Flour
½	Cup Dutch Process Cocoa Powder
¼	Teaspoon Salt
½	Cup Dark or Semi-Sweet Chocolate Chips

Crumb-Topped Brownies

Lace Sugar Crisps

Simple, sweet, and crunchy, these caramelized disks make a gorgeous addition to parfaits or even a simple dish of dairy-free "ice cream." A smear of chocolate ganache pressed between two cookies will give you a delicious confection with ease. Of course, if you are really handy, you could let them cool over a spoon handle or curved surface to form tuiles. Better yet, twirl them all the way around into a tube and make cannoli shells! I prefer to keep it simple, but these crisps are a great medium to play around with. Their distinctive structure makes them similar to a delicate topping of spun sugar.

¼	Cup Margarine
¼	Cup Dark Brown Sugar
¼	Cup Dark Agave Nectar
¼	Cup All-Purpose Flour
	Dash Salt

Preheat your oven to 375°F (190°C) and line two baking sheets with silpats or parchment paper.

Heat the margarine, sugar, and agave nectar together in a small saucepan over medium-low heat. Remove from the heat once the margarine is completely melted, and vigorously whisk in the flour and salt to avoid clumps.

Drop about ½ teaspoon of batter per cookie onto your prepared baking sheets. Take care to place them several inches apart, as they spread like crazy. Bake the crisps for 5 to 6 minutes, until they are caramelized and bubbly, but be sure to keep a close eye on them while they are in the oven. Wait a few minutes for the crisps to cool and solidify before handling. They are very fragile after they harden, so be gentle! Cool the cookies completely on a wire rack, and store them in an airtight container at room temperature. Heat and moisture will change their texture, so the crisps may remain slightly soft if you are baking in a very humid climate.

Makes Approximately 48 Crisps

Lace Sugar Crisps

Maple Pistachio Crèmes

Pistachio fan that I am, I find it frustrating that this beautiful nut is so rarely utilized by most home cooks. Flavorful and agreeable with a cornucopia of other flavors, be it sweet or savory, the hardest part about working with these shelled treasures is choosing what else to pair them with! In this case, I really wanted the pistachio to finally get its fair share of the spotlight, accentuating it with the rounded, mellow sweetness of maple syrup. Crunchy, creamy, and with a lurid green hue that artificial colors cannot even touch, these cookies could make a pistachio lover out of anyone.

If a food processor is not within your grasp, feel free to substitute ⅔ cup of pistachio butter for the 1 cup of pistachios. With your store bought pistachio butter in hand, the remainder of the crème can be whipped up in a blender, rather than a food processor. Though not as common as some of the other nut "butters," pistachio butter can be found in select natural food stores or online.

Preheat your oven to 350°F (175°C) and line two baking sheets with silpats or parchment paper.

In a large microwave-safe bowl, melt the margarine and then stir in the maple syrup. Add in 2 cups of the flour, along with the baking powder, vanilla, and salt. Stir the batter until all of the ingredients are fully combined. Add in the remainder of the flour, and combine. The batter should be rather thick, so resist the temptation to add more liquid! Scoop out walnut-sized balls and roll them in your hands to make them nicely rounded. Place the balls onto your prepared baking sheets about 1 inch apart. Bake for 10 to 12 minutes, but don't wait for them to brown. Once the cookies firm up a bit, and no longer appear moist on top, they are done! Let the cookies cool on the sheets.

To make the pistachio crème, toss the pistachios into your food processor and pulverize them for up to 10 minutes, so that they become relatively smooth and paste-like. With the motor running, drizzle in the soy creamer, followed by the maple syrup and vanilla. Process until completely combined and smooth. Once the cookies are fully cooled, drop a dollop of the crème (about 1 to 2 teaspoons) onto the flat side of one cookie, and top with a second cookie. Repeat with the remaining cookies.

Makes 12 to 18 Sandwich Cookies

Cookies:

½	Cup Margarine
⅔	Cup Maple Syrup
2¾	Cups All-Purpose Flour
1	Teaspoon Baking Powder
1	Teaspoon Vanilla Extract
¼	Teaspoon Salt

Pistachio Crème:

1	Cup Shelled Raw Pistachios or
	⅔ cup Pistachio Butter
¼	Cup Plain Soy Creamer
3	Tablespoons Maple Syrup
½	Teaspoon Vanilla

Maple Pistachio Crèmes

Nut Case Cookies

I often buy huge bags of nuts at a time, which is great for larger recipes, but when I get down to the bottom there is little that they can do to complete a dish alone. That is where the idea for these cookies originated. Utilizing all of those remnants, I have created a delightfully crunchy variant on my typical chocolate chip cookie dough. Although this is my favorite combination and I highly recommend it, this recipe was meant to use up scraps, so feel free to substitute whatever whole or chopped nuts you have on hand. You could even go a bit 'nuts' and throw in some almond extract!

1	Cup Margarine
½	Cup Granulated Sugar
½	Cup Dark Brown Sugar
1	Cup Whole Wheat Pastry Flour
1½	Cups All-Purpose Flour
1	Teaspoon Baking Soda
½	Teaspoon Salt
1	Teaspoon Vanilla Extract
¼	Cup Plain Soy Creamer
½	Cup Almonds
½	Cup Cashews
½	Cup Pistachios

Preheat your oven to 350°F (175°C) and line two baking sheets with silpats or parchment paper.

In your stand mixer, cream together the margarine and both sugars. Combine the flours, baking soda, and salt in a separate bowl. Slowly add the flour mixture to your mixer until everything is combined. Add the vanilla and soy creamer. Mix so that the dough is completely homogeneous through and through. Fold in the nuts by hand to distribute evenly.

Drop rounded tablespoons of dough onto your prepared baking sheets, allowing plenty of room for them to spread. Bake for 10 to 14 minutes, until the cookies are no longer shiny. Remove them from the baking sheet immediately and allow them to cool.

Makes 36 Cookies

Nut Case Cookies

Orange Hazelnut Biscotti

Sometimes my recipes are born out of simple flavor combinations that just sound good together, without knowing what specific dessert they might find their way into. This recipe was just such a creation. Late one night, hazelnut, orange, and chocolate danced across my mind, begging to be joined in reality. I don't remember exactly why these elements ended up as biscotti, but let me tell you, the delicious results prove that it was clearly meant to be.

½	Cup Margarine
¾	Cup Granulated Sugar
1	Tablespoon Flax Seeds
2	Tablespoons Water
	Juice (About ¼ Cup) and
	Zest of 1 Orange
2	Cups All-Purpose Flour
1½	Teaspoons Baking Powder
¼	Teaspoon Salt
½	Cup Chopped Hazelnuts
4½	Ounces Dark Chocolate

Preheat your oven to 350°F (175°C) and line a baking sheet with a silpat or parchment paper.

Cream the margarine in your mixer until light and fluffy in texture. Add in the sugar, beating until fully incorporated. Grind the flax seeds into a powder with a spice grinder, and whiz them together with the water to form a paste. Add the flax seed mixture to your mixer, stirring well. Toss in the zest from your orange and mix again. Sift in the flour, baking powder, and salt, mixing lightly until relatively combined. Continuing with the mixer on a slow speed, dump in the hazelnuts, and slowly juice your orange into the mixture until it just comes together. It may take more or less juice, depending on the variety of orange you use and how well you can squeeze your fruit! If the dough is still crumbly, grab another orange and extract just enough juice so that everything comes together.

Shape the resulting dough into a long, skinny rectangle about 1 inch tall by 2 inches wide by however long that ends up, and place it onto your prepared baking sheet. Slide the baking sheet into the oven for 35 to 40 minutes.

The top of the biscotti loaf should be lightly browned, but don't panic if it seems a little bit soft and bread-like on the inside. Cool the biscotti for at least 5 minutes, and slice horizontally into cookies that are about ½ inch thick. Lay the slices down flat on one of their cut sides on the baking sheet, and return the biscotti to the oven for another 10 minutes. Turn the slices over onto their other cut side and bake for another 10 minutes. Allow the biscotti to cool completely.

Place the chocolate in a relatively shallow, microwave-safe dish that can accommodate the full length of your biscotti. In the microwave, melt your chocolate in 30-second intervals until it is completely smooth, stirring well after each interval. Dip one cookie into the chocolate and place it back on a silpat or parchment paper. Repeat this process with each cookie. Allow the biscotti to dry completely before moving them again.

Makes 12 to 15 Biscotti

Orange Hazelnut Biscotti

Party Mix Bars

Are some friends coming over for a movie night, game of scrabble, video games, or just to hang out? Don't drag out that tired old bag of snack mix; whip up a batch of party mix bars! This sweet and salty treat comes in an easy-to-grab square, rather than a handful of loose munchies, so there will be less mess for you to clean up later. Plus, making a batch large enough to satisfy the most ravenous visitors is no more difficult than preparing crispy rice treats. So what are you waiting for? When they find out what's baking, your guests will arrive any minute!

2	Cups Mini Pretzel Twists
2	Cups Chex® Rice Cereal
3	Cups Crispy Rice Cereal
1½	Cups Mixed Nuts
1	Tablespoon Margarine
¾	Cup Granulated Sugar
1	Cup Light Corn Syrup
1	Teaspoon Vanilla Extract

Combine the pretzels, both cereals, and nuts in a large bowl. Liberally coat a 9 x 13 inch baking pan with cooking spray. Set both aside.

Set a medium saucepan over low heat and begin by melting the margarine alone. Once it has liquefied, add in the sugar and syrup, stirring as necessary until the sugar crystals dissolve. Turn up the heat and bring the mixture to a steady boil. Cook for an additional 3 to 5 minutes, until it appears to have thickened slightly. Remove from the heat and quickly stir in the vanilla. Pour the contents of your saucepan over the dry mix and fold it in carefully but briskly, being careful not to crush the cereal.

Pour everything into your prepared pan and gently press it out into an even layer. Let cool completely before cutting into bars.

Makes 20 to 24 Bars

Party Mix Bars

Peanut Butter Bombs

They may look like plain old chocolate cookies from the outside, but one bite will reveal an explosion of creamy peanut butter! Seriously satisfying, like a peanut butter cup in cookie-form, these are perhaps the only bomb that I can condone making.

Peanut Butter Filling:

¼	Cup Creamy Peanut Butter
⅓	Cup Confectioner's Sugar
1	Teaspoon Plain Soymilk

Chocolate Cookie:

¼	Cup Margarine
¼	Cup Creamy Peanut Butter
⅓	Cup Dark Brown Sugar
⅓	Cup Granulated Sugar
6	Ounces Vanilla Soy Yogurt
1	Tablespoon Plain Soymilk
1	Teaspoon Vanilla Extract
1¼	Cups All-Purpose Flour
½	Cup Dutch Process Cocoa Powder
¼	Teaspoon Baking Soda
¼	Teaspoon Salt

Preheat your oven to 350°F (175°C) and line two baking sheets with silpats or parchment paper.

In a small bowl, combine all of the ingredients for the filling and stir well. It should have a crumbly consistency, but still hold together when pressed. Once everything is fully incorporated, set aside.

In your mixer, cream together the margarine, peanut butter, and both sugars. Mix in the soy yogurt, soymilk, and vanilla, and continue beating until smooth. In a separate bowl, combine the flour, cocoa, baking soda, and salt. Slowly add these dry ingredients into the wet, being careful not to over mix.

The dough may be rather sticky. If you have a problem shaping it, let the dough sit in the refrigerator for about 30 minutes, or try moistening your hands slightly before handling.

For each cookie, roll about a tablespoon of dough into a ball and press it down flat onto your silpat or parchment paper. Line the cookies up 3 x 3 on your two baking sheets, with plenty of room in between. Drop a rounded teaspoon or so of your peanut butter filling into the center of each, and top with another flattened round of dough. Be sure to cover the whole dollop of filling, and check to see that the edges meet all around the cookie. Bake for 8 to 12 minutes, until the cookies no longer appear shiny on top. Remove the cookies from the oven, and allow them to cool on the baking sheet.

Makes 18 Cookies

Peanut Butter Bombs

Peanut-Plus Cookies

All of the signs would seem to say that these are your typical tasty peanut butter cookies: full of nutty flavor, soft and chewy, yet still satisfyingly crisp. Certainly every aspect of this classification is accurate, although there is something slightly different about these cookies that most people would not even venture to guess. Lentils are ground up and added to the mix, in place of the traditional wheat flour, to make an authentic gluten-free goodie. Before you write these off as some terrible mistake, just try them for yourself. Even the most unexpected ingredients, if used in the right way, can create something amazing.

½	Cup Red Lentils, Dry
½	Cup Plain Soymilk
¼	Cup Instant Mashed Potato Flakes
1	Cup Crunchy Peanut Butter
¾	Cup Granulated Sugar
¼	Cup Cornstarch
2	Teaspoons Cream of Tartar
1	Teaspoon Baking Soda
1	Teaspoon Vanilla Extract
¼	Teaspoon Salt

Preheat your oven to 350°F (175°C) and line two baking sheets with silpats or parchment paper.

Begin by grinding up your dry lentils in a food processor for a good 5 to 10 minutes, until they become a fine powder. This step is crucial, as any remaining pieces of whole lentils will contribute a slightly off texture to the finished cookies. If you do not have a food processor handy, then the lentils can be ground in a spice grinder in about two batches.

While your lentils are churning away, combine the soymilk and mashed potato flakes in a microwave-safe bowl and heat for one minute. Let the potato mixture cool for a minute or two, and toss it into a stand mixer along with your freshly processed lentil flour. Mix in the peanut butter and sugar. Sprinkle in the cornstarch while keeping your mixer at a low speed, bringing it up faster once everything is well combined and no longer threatens to send starch flying out. Make sure that the dough is thoroughly mixed at this point, as lumps of cornstarch do not make for tasty cookies. Add in the remaining ingredients and combine.

Spoon rounded tablespoons of dough onto the prepared baking sheets. Leave a good amount of room between the cookies to allow for spreading, but they shouldn't go too far. Slide the dough lumps into the oven and cook for 10 to 12 minutes, until they are no longer shiny on top, but have not yet begun to brown around the edges. In order to ensure a soft, chewy cookie, remove the cookies from the oven just before they begin to take on color. Allow them to sit on the hot tray for another 5 minutes before pulling the silpat off onto a cooler surface.

Makes 24 Cookies

Peanut-Plus Cookies

Pfeffernusse

Rather than baking another batch of those tired old gingersnaps, add some excitement to your holiday lineup with this traditional German cookie. Relying more on anise than cinnamon, these sugarcoated cookies have a distinct licorice bite, accompanied by a good deal of spice. You may find it difficult to sacrifice any of these delights to leave out for Santa, let alone share with your friends!

½　Cup Margarine
½　Cup Granulated Sugar
2　Tablespoons Molasses
1　Tablespoon Canola or
　　Vegetable Oil
2　Tablespoons Plain or Vanilla Soymilk
¾　Teaspoon Pure Anise Extract or
　　½ Teaspoon Ground Anise
1¼　Cups All-Purpose Flour
½　Cup Almond Meal
1　Teaspoon Baking Powder
¼　Teaspoon Baking Soda
¼　Teaspoon Salt
¾　Teaspoon Ground Cinnamon
¼　Teaspoon Ground Cloves
¼　Teaspoon Ground Cardamom
⅛–¼　Teaspoon Ground Black Pepper
　　Confectioner's Sugar to Coat

In your stand mixer, cream the margarine and sugar together until light and fluffy. Scrape down the side of the bowl to prevent any lumps from being left behind. Beat in the molasses, oil, and soymilk, followed shortly by the anise extract.

Combine the flour, almond meal, baking powder, baking soda, salt, and dry spices in a large bowl. Gradually add this flour mixture into the wet ingredients. Stir slowly until a cohesive dough begins to form, so that the dry ingredients do not threaten to fly out and decorate your kitchen walls. Manually press the dough into a ball and wrap it in plastic wrap before tossing it into the refrigerator for at least 30 minutes.

When it is time to remove the dough from the refrigerator, preheat your oven to 350°F (175°C) and line two baking sheets with silpats or parchment paper.

Roll the dough into 1-inch balls, handling it as little as possible. Place the spheres about two inches apart on your prepared baking sheets. Bake for 10 to 12 minutes, until the cookies turn an even, light brown color.

Once they come out of the oven, roll the cookies in a dish full of confectioner's sugar and cool them on a wire rack. The cookies may absorb the sugar, so you might wish to coat them a second time to achieve the same look.

Makes 48 Cookies

Pfeffernusse

Sesame Oatmeal Cookies

So few sweets promote sesame as a featured flavor, and I think this is a real shame. The wonderful nutty taste and toothsome texture that sesame brings to the party is so unique that nothing else tastes quite like it. Using the whole seeds in conjunction with tahini gives you the best of both worlds… a chewy cookie that still has a nice crunch every now and then. Add in some hearty rolled oats, and you have one seriously satisfying snack.

1	Cup Granulated Sugar
1	Cup Whole Wheat Flour
1	Teaspoon Baking Soda
½	Teaspoon Salt
½	Teaspoon Cinnamon
1	Cup Rolled Oats
½	Cup Sesame Seeds
½	Cup Unsweetened Applesauce
1	Ripe, Medium-Sized Banana
2	Tablespoons Plain Soymilk
¼	Cup Canola or Vegetable Oil
1	Cup Tahini
2	Teaspoons Molasses
1	Teaspoon Vanilla Extract

Preheat your oven to 350°F (175°C) and line two baking sheets with silpats or parchment paper.

In a medium bowl, sift together the sugar, flour, baking soda, salt, and cinnamon. Stir in the oats and sesame seeds. Set aside.

In a blender, combine the applesauce, banana, soymilk, and oil. Process on high until completely smooth. Throw this mixture into your stand mixer along with the tahini, and combine thoroughly. Mix in the molasses and vanilla. Slowly add the oat/flour mixture in a number of small installments, to avoid spraying flour everywhere.

Drop rounded spoonfuls of the dough onto your prepared baking sheets. Flatten the tops by lightly pressing with your fingers, but don't worry if they are very sticky and won't smooth out perfectly. Bake for 12 to 15 minutes until the cookies are no longer shiny on top, but have not yet begun to brown around the edges. In order to ensure a soft, chewy cookie, remove the cookies from the oven just before they begin taking on color. Allow the cookies to cool for a few minutes on the sheet, before moving them to a wire rack. Store them in an airtight container.

Makes 24 to 36 Cookies

Sesame Oatmeal Cookies

Strawberry Spirals

Everyone is familiar with the standard cast of characters that occupy a spread of festive holiday cookies, as they rarely deviate from the traditional. Sure, the chocolate pinwheel that graces many of these platters is a perfectly agreeable shortbread, but it is all too often lacking in either chocolate or vanilla flavor, cursed to forever remain a lovely but terribly bland piece of eye-candy. Rather than sacrificing taste for design, why not roll up some flavorful fruit, like brilliant red strawberries? Trust me, these cookies will leave the conventional version in the dust!

Fruit Filling:

2	Cups Dried Strawberries or Other Dried Fruit
⅓	Cup Water
1	Teaspoon Cornstarch

Cookie Dough:

½	Cup Margarine
½	Cup Vegetable Shortening
½	Cup Granulated Sugar
1	Teaspoon Vanilla Extract
2¼	Cups All-Purpose Flour
½	Cup Whole Wheat Pastry Flour
¼	Teaspoon Baking Powder
¼	Teaspoon Baking Soda
¼	Teaspoon Salt
⅓–½	Cup Plain Soy Creamer

In your food processor or blender, blend together the dried strawberries and water until mostly smooth. Slowly sprinkle in the cornstarch with the motor running, in order to prevent lumps from forming. Set aside.

In your stand mixer, cream together the margarine, vegetable shortening, and sugar until light and fluffy. Mix in the vanilla and beat until fully combined. In a separate bowl, whisk together the flours, baking powder, baking soda, and salt. Slowly add this flour mixture to your batter, and mix just until combined. Drizzle in the soy creamer until the dough achieves a workable consistency. It should be very stiff and firm, but moist enough to hold together when pressed. Divide the dough into two even halves and form each into a rectangle as best you can. Wrap the rectangles in plastic wrap, and let them rest in the refrigerator for at least 2 hours.

Once thoroughly chilled, remove one piece of dough from the refrigerator and roll it out between two sheets of parchment paper to about ¼ inch thick. Try to keep it as rectangular as possible. Peel away one piece of the parchment and gently spread the strawberry mixture atop your dough, leaving about ½ inch border without fruit around edges. Starting with a long side of the dough, roll it into a log, using the parchment as leverage, and being careful not to mash the filling. Repeat this process with the second rectangle. Re-wrap these logs in plastic wrap and chill in the freezer for another few hours, until solid but pliable. I find that the dough will hold its shape better if you stick it inside a cardboard paper towel roll that has been split down the middle, but it should be okay even if you don't go to this trouble.

Once the dough is properly chilled, preheat your oven to 350°F (175°C) and line two baking sheets with silpats or fresh parchment paper. Using a serrated knife carefully cut the logs crosswise into ⅓ to ½ inch thick slices. Use a sawing motion with the knife, and try not to apply significant pressure. Place the slices on the prepared baking sheets with a good amount of room around them, about an inch or so. Bake for 15 to 17 minutes, until the cookies just begin to lightly brown around the edges. Remove from the oven, and let the cookies sit for one additional minute before transferring them to a wire rack for further cooling.

Makes 36 to 48 Cookies

Strawberry Spirals

Turtle Shortbread Wedges

If you ask me, rich dark chocolate, sweet caramel and crunchy pecans were simply made for each other. The name of "turtle" for this fabulous trio came from candies that were sort of shaped like the animal. Honestly, I have never understood why you would want to eat a turtle in the first place, even if it was a sweet confection. Name aside, my interpretation of the traditional "turtle" ingredients is a real knockout. This decadent assemblage has been known to elicit moans of pleasure just upon first sight. A full batch won't last long no matter how many people you choose to share with (or not), so proceed with caution!

Preheat your oven to 350°F (175°C) and generously grease an 8 inch round cake pan.

For the shortbread, cream the margarine and both sugars together in your stand mixer until soft and fluffy. Add in the vanilla and salt. Turn the mixer off to add in both the flour and cocoa, and start it up on a very slow speed so that the dry ingredients do not fly out. It may take a little bit of mixing for everything to come together, but be patient and give it time. Press the dough into the bottom of your prepared pan. It will be very sticky so you may want to grease your hands or use a piece of wax paper to smooth it in, but either way be sure to cover the bottom of the pan evenly and completely. Bake for 20 to 22 minutes, until the dough appears firmer on top, and the sides look a bit crispy. If you are not sure if it is done by that time, just take it out anyway. It is hard to distinguish "done" from "burnt" on this one.

While the shortbread is finishing off in the oven, you can begin to prepare the caramel topping. Take out a medium saucepan and place your sugar, cream of tartar, salt, and water inside. Set it over medium heat and stir the mixture just to combine, after which time you must resist the urge to agitate it for about 5 to 7 more minutes. Once it turns a shade of light amber, it will continue to color very quickly, so stay on your toes! (At this point, your shortbread should be out of the oven and nearby, ready to go) Stir occasionally until it reaches the hard-crack stage of 300°F (150°C). If you don't have a candy thermometer handy, drop a small amount of the syrup into a cup of cold water to test. It should form thin, brittle threads that break if you try to bend them. Stand back from the stove slightly while still stirring, and pour in the soy creamer with care, as it could splash back up. Stir in the pecans just to combine, turn off the heat, and pour the whole mixture over the chocolate shortbread.

Return the pan to your oven for 10 more minutes, until the caramel has darkened slightly. Let it cool for about 20 minutes before running a knife around the edge to loosen. Turn the cookie disk out onto a cutting board, and cut into wedges while it is still slightly warm.

Makes 16 Cookies

Chocolate Shortbread:

¾	Cup Margarine
¼	Cup Dark Brown Sugar
2	Tablespoons Granulated Sugar
1	Teaspoon Vanilla Extract
	Pinch Salt
1	Cup All-Purpose Flour
¼	Cup Dutch Process Cocoa Powder

Caramel Topping:

2	Cups Granulated Sugar
¼	Teaspoon Cream of Tartar
	Pinch Salt
⅓	Cup Water
¼	Cup Plain Soy Creamer
1¼	Cups Lightly Toasted Pecan Halves

Turtle Shortbread Wedges

Whoopie Pies

Wrapped up in plastic like hazardous material, and sporting ingredient lists that read more like failed science experiments than food, I have never understood why mass-produced sweets such as the traditional whoopie pie are considered an improvement over home baking. Still, that does not mean the concept itself isn't alluring. Two soft chocolate cookies with a creamy vanilla frosting sandwiched in between can seem like a dream to any student perusing the offerings in their cafeteria. It wasn't long before I thought to try replicating this old favorite, but as a dessert suitable for both young and more mature taste buds. By making it yourself, fillers and artificial flavors never even enter the picture, so you can discover what a whoopie pie should really taste like.

Chocolate Cookies:

1	Cup Plain Soymilk
1	Teaspoon Apple Cider Vinegar
1	Cup Whole Wheat Pastry Flour
1	Cup All-Purpose Flour
½	Cup Dutch Process Cocoa Powder
1	Teaspoon Baking Powder
1	Teaspoon Baking Soda
1	Teaspoon Salt
½	Cup Margarine
¼	Cup Granulated Sugar
½	Cup Dark Brown Sugar
2	Tablespoons Vegan "Sour Cream"
1	Teaspoon Vanilla Extract

Crème Filling:

2	Cups Confectioner's Sugar
⅓	Cup Vegetable Shortening
3	Tablespoons Plain Soymilk
1	Teaspoon Vanilla Extract

Preheat your oven to 350°F (175°C) and line two baking sheets with silpats or parchment paper.

In a small bowl, whisk together the soymilk and vinegar and set aside, allowing the mixture time to curdle. In a medium bowl, whisk together the flours, cocoa, baking powder, baking soda, and salt. Set aside.

Over in your stand mixer, cream together the margarine and both sugars, beating to ensure that the contents of the bowl are creamy and fully combined. Add the "sour cream" and mix again until smooth.

Returning to the now curdled soymilk, whisk in the vanilla. Beginning with these wet ingredients, alternately add them with the dry ingredients into your mixer. Scrape down the sides as necessary, and beat the mixture just enough to fully combine.

Use an ice cream scoop or measuring cup to drop 3 to 4 tablespoons of dough at a time onto your prepared baking sheets. Leave a good amount of space between each cookie, about 2 inches, allowing them room to spread a bit. Bake for 10 to 14 minutes, until they crackle slightly on top. Remove the cookies from the oven and let them cool completely on the baking sheets where they should firm up a bit more.

To make the filling, begin with the mixer on low and beat together the confectioner's sugar and shortening. Add the soymilk, and finally the vanilla. Once the sugar has become incorporated, turn the mixer up to high and whip for a good 2 or 3 minutes; this will incorporate more air, making for a lighter, fluffier filling.

Drop a healthy dollop of the crème mixture onto the flat side of one cooled cookie, and place a second cookie on top. Press down gently to bring the filling right out to the edge. Repeat this process with your remaining cookies and crème filling.

Makes 8 to 10 Sandwich Cookies

Whoopie Pies

CAKES & CUPCAKES

Apple Spice Cake

My Nana always goes above and beyond the call of duty to celebrate my special occasions, so when her birthday rolled around, I wanted to seize the opportunity to return the favor. There was just one problem; she is diabetic. How was I to make her a sweet treat, when sweets by definition were all but off limits? By avoiding the addition of overly refined sugars and flours, of course! This cake gets all of its sweetness through fruit sugars. When it was served on the day of my Nana's party, it was wolfed down with immense enthusiasm. Even the kids dug in with voracious appetites, despite the more mature flavors and lack of neon-colored frosting.

Of course the severity of diabetes will differ from one person to another. Make sure to check that this cake will still be appropriate for anyone you may be serving it to who has dietary restrictions.

Preheat your oven to 350°F (175°C) and grease two 8 inch round cake pans.

Combine the flour, oats, spices, baking powder, baking soda, and salt in a large bowl and set aside. In your stand mixer, cream the margarine to soften it a bit before adding in the concentrated juice, followed by the applesauce and vanilla. Mix well; it might look a bit lumpy, but be patient, as it will take on a more enticing appearance shortly!

With your mixer on low speed, to avoid sending flour flying onto the walls, slowly add in the dry ingredients residing in your large bowl. Be careful not to over mix. Finally, fold in your apple pieces, raisins, and nuts by hand. Once these additions are well distributed, spread the batter into your greased pans. It makes for a very thick batter, so you may have to press it into shape with a spatula to evenly fill each pan. Bake for 25 to 30 minutes, until a toothpick inserted into the center of each layer comes out clean.

Let the layers cool to room temperature inside the pans. Turn the first layer out onto the plate you want to serve it on, and spread all of the apple butter on top. Smooth it out almost to the edge but not quite, as the weight of the top layer will press it out further. Place the second layer on top and have a taste of sweetness without the sugar rush!

Makes 10 to 12 Servings

Apple Spice Cake:
2	Cups Whole Wheat Pastry Flour
2	Cups Rolled Oats
2	Teaspoons Ground Cinnamon
½	Teaspoon Ground Nutmeg
½	Teaspoon Ground Cloves
1	Teaspoon Baking Powder
1½	Teaspoons Baking Soda
½	Teaspoon Salt
½	Cup Margarine
1⅓	Cups Apple Juice Concentrate, Thawed and Undiluted
½	Cup Unsweetened Applesauce
2	Teaspoons Vanilla Extract
2	Apples, Peeled, Cored, and Diced
1	Cup Raisins
1	Cup Chopped Walnuts

Topping:
1	Cup Apple Butter

Apple Spice Cake

Bananas Foster Cake

Banana cake is often a disappointing, dry mess as many people think it's perfectly all right to use any old banana bread recipe, slap some frosting on top, and call it a cake. Step it up a notch with a sweet treat that is actually meant to be a dessert, and you will understand what a huge difference it makes. Modeled after the traditional flavors of bananas foster, the layers are soaked in rum before assembly and topped with a caramel frosting that pulls the whole dessert together. In the typical showy fashion of traditional bananas foster, the banana slices used for garnish could be made with the addition of some rum, and then set ablaze to let the alcohol cook off. Knowing my personal ineptitude with fire, I think it is safer to recommend a simple sauté. The end results are still extraordinary, even without the stovetop bonfire.

Banana Cake:

2½	Cups All-Purpose Flour
2	Teaspoons Baking Powder
2	Teaspoons Baking Soda
½	Teaspoon Salt
⅔	Cup Plain Soymilk
1	Teaspoon Apple Cider Vinegar
½	Cup Margarine
¾	Cup Granulated Sugar
½	Cup Dark Brown Sugar
5	Ripe, Medium-Sized Bananas
1	Tablespoon Vanilla Extract
6	Tablespoons Rum (Any Variety)

Caramel Frosting:

1	Cup Margarine
3½	Cups Confectioner's Sugar
⅓	Cup Brown Sugar
1½	Teaspoons Water
1	Teaspoon Vanilla Extract

Sautéed Bananas:

1	Firm, Large Banana, sliced into ¼ inch rounds
2	Tablespoons Brown Sugar
1	Tablespoon Water

Preheat your oven to 350°F (175°C) and lightly grease and flour two 8 inch round cake pans.

In a small bowl, whisk together the flour, baking powder, baking soda, and salt, and set aside. In a separate small bowl, combine the soymilk and vinegar, also moving this to the side.

In your stand mixer, cream together the margarine and both sugars until light and fluffy. Mash the bananas well and mix them in, along with the vanilla. Add the flour mixture, alternately with your now curdled soymilk, into your mixer. Ensure that everything is fully combined before equally dividing the batter between your two prepared pans.

Bake for 25 to 30 minutes, until a toothpick inserted into the center of each layer comes out clean. Remove from the oven, and while they are still warm, poke the cake tops numerous times with your testing toothpick. Evenly pour 3 tablespoons of the rum over each of the layers. Let the cake layers cool completely before turning them out of the pans to frost.

For the frosting, cream the margarine well and incorporate the confectioner's sugar slowly. Microwave the brown sugar together with the water for approximately 30 to 60 seconds, just until the sugar dissolves and it begins to bubble a bit. Let the brown sugar stand for a few minutes to cool off, then pour it into the margarine mixture. With the mixer on high, beat the frosting vigorously until all of the ingredients are fully incorporated. Stir in the vanilla, and frost the cake as desired.

For the banana garnish, combine the brown sugar and water in a non-stick skillet over medium heat. Cook until the sugar dissolves. Add the banana, and stir to coat all of the pieces well. Cook for about 2 minutes, until the sugar bubbles and darkens into a golden caramel, stirring gently every so often. Remove the bananas from the skillet and transfer them to a silpat. Separate each slice so that they do not stick together. Let them cool completely before garnishing the cake.

Makes 10 to 12 Servings

Bananas Foster Cake

Canine Cake

My dog is just as important as any other member of our family, so whenever her birthday comes up, I like to treat her to something special. This particular cake happens to be her personal favorite, judging by the way she inhales it; in mere minutes the entire thing is reduced to a few errant crumbs, which inevitably find their way into her mouth as well! You can even enjoy this cake with your lucky pup, since it is made with ingredients that are also perfectly agreeable to a human palate. Think of it as a dense peanut butter carrot cake, if you will. If you are still a beginner baker, then this is the perfect recipe to start with, as I am certain that your dog will be your most easily pleased critic!

Preheat your oven to 350°F (175°C) and lightly grease a medium sized ramekin or any 8-ounce oven-safe bowl.

Combine the flour and baking soda in a medium bowl. Stir in the carrot bits. Add the remaining wet ingredients, and mix well. The batter will be very thick, similar to cookie dough. Drop the batter into your prepared ramekin and bake for 25 to 35 minutes, until a toothpick inserted into the center comes out clean. Let cool completely before serving, so that your dog doesn't burn his or her mouth!

Makes 1 Small Cake

½	Cup All-Purpose Flour
½	Teaspoon Baking Soda
½	Cup Shredded Carrots
2	Tablespoons Peanut Butter
2	Tablespoons Canola or Vegetable Oil
¼	Cup Unsweetened Applesauce

Canine Cake

Caramel Macchiato "Cheese" Cake

Coffee in general is a favorite flavor and beverage of mine. Yet, while the wide array of gourmet coffee drinks always sound so enticing, the vegan options from which I can choose are sadly limited. After leaving so many cafés empty handed, I decided to turn my greatest craving into cake! As aromatic as a coffee shop, and dressed with a vanilla and caramel topping, this cake is a spitting image of the original. Now you can have your coffee and eat it, too!

Preheat your oven to 350°F (175°C) and lightly grease a 9 inch springform pan.

Place the cookie crumbs in a medium bowl and pour the melted margarine on top. Add the salt, stirring to thoroughly coat all of the crumbs, and dump this mixture into your prepared pan. Use your palms to firmly press the crumbs down, taking care to completely cover the bottom. Bake for approximately 10 minutes and let cool, leaving the oven on.

For the main body of the cake, drain the package of tofu before tossing it into your food processor or blender to purée. Once smooth, add in the "cream cheese" and sugar, processing again to combine. In a small dish, stir the coffee powder into the liqueur to dissolve all of the granules. Add this mixture into your food processor or blender, and process to combine. Add the vanilla and salt, scrape the sides to make sure you are not leaving anything out of the mix, and process one last time to completely blend all of the ingredients. Pour the mixture into your pan and tap gently on a flat surface to release any air bubbles trapped below the surface. Smooth down the top with a spatula, and bake for 20 minutes. After that amount of time, lower the oven temperature to 325°F (160°C). Bake for an additional 20 to 25 minutes, until the cake is still a bit wobbly in the center but slightly darker in color.

As the cake finishes baking, stir together the "sour cream," vanilla, and sugar in a small bowl until smooth. Once the cake comes out of the oven, pour this layer over the top, and smooth it down to achieve an even covering. Bake once more for 5 to 10 minutes, just until bubbles begin to percolate around the edges. The cake will still seem rather loose and wobbly, but it will continue to set up as it cools. Let it come to room temperature before making the caramel drizzle.

To complete the cake, set a saucepan on the stove and gently melt the margarine over medium heat. Once liquefied, add in the brown sugar, soymilk, and salt. Whisking slowly and steadily, bring the mixture to a gentle boil and continue to cook for about 5 minutes. Stir in half of the arrowroot and whisk thoroughly to prevent lumps. Cook for one more minute, remove from heat, and add in the remainder of the arrowroot, whisking rapidly once more. Let the sauce cool for at least 10 minutes before pouring it over the cake in a checkerboard pattern, or as desired.

Makes 12 to 16 Servings

Chocolate Crust:
1½	Cups Chocolate Wafer Cookie Crumbs
¼	Cup Margarine
¼	Teaspoon Salt

Coffee "Cheese" Cake:
1	12-Ounce Package Extra-Firm Silken Tofu
2	8-Ounce Packages Vegan "Cream Cheese"
⅔	Cup Granulated Sugar
2	Tablespoons Instant Coffee Powder
¼	Cup Kahlua® or Coffee Liqueur
1	Teaspoon Vanilla Extract
	Pinch Salt

Vanilla Topping:
1	Cup Vegan "Sour Cream"
1	Tablespoon Vanilla Extract
¼	Cup Granulated Sugar

Caramel Sauce:
2	Tablespoons Margarine, Melted
⅓	Cup Dark Brown Sugar
2	Tablespoon Plain Soymilk
¼	Teaspoon Salt
1	Teaspoon Arrowroot Powder

Caramel Macchiato "Cheese" Cake

Chai "Cheese" Cake

I just love the spicy nuances of chai tea, but this exotic flavor can be difficult to find in commercial sweets and recipes for homemade baked goods alike. Those that do attempt this delicate balance of sweet and spicy often fail miserably, creating a terribly watered-down final product by using only weak brewed tea. Now you can have all the piquant flavors of chai without diluting your dessert. This "cheese" cake uses substantial amounts of real ground spices to impart an intense flavor that is sure to please even the most discriminating chai enthusiasts, such as myself.

Preheat your oven to 375°F (190°C) degrees and lightly grease and flour a 9 inch round springform pan.

Toss the graham cracker crumbs into a medium bowl. Pour the melted margarine and brown rice syrup over the crumbs and stir to combine. Using your hands, press the mixture into the bottom of your prepared pan, bringing it only about ¼ inch further up the sides, to form a small lip at the edge of the crust. Set aside.

For the filling, drain the tofu of any excess water and blend it in your food processor or blender until smooth. Add in the "cream cheese" and blend. Scrape down the sides and blend again, ensuring that no lumps remain. Incorporate the sugar, spices, and salt. Scrape down the sides once more, checking for any concentrated pockets of spice. Blend thoroughly to create a homogeneous mixture, and pour it on top of your graham cracker crust. Tap the whole pan on the counter lightly, to even it out and eliminate any air bubbles. Smooth the top with your spatula before transferring it to the oven. Bake for approximately 30 minutes, until the sides begin to pull away from the pan and the center still appears to be rather wobbly when tapped. Trust me; it will become firmer in time!

Let the cake cool completely before moving it into the refrigerator, where I suggest you let it chill for at least 12 to 24 hours before serving. This will allow the flavors to fully develop and intensify.

Makes 12 to 16 Servings

Graham Cracker Crust:

2½	Cups Vegan Graham Cracker Crumbs
⅓	Cup Margarine, Melted
1	Tablespoon Brown Rice Syrup

Chai Filling:

1	12-Ounce Package Extra-Firm Silken Tofu
2	8-Ounce Packages Vegan "Cream Cheese"
1	Cup Granulated Sugar
2	Teaspoons Ground Ginger
1½	Teaspoons Ground Coriander
1	Teaspoon Ground Cinnamon
½	Teaspoon Ground Allspice
¼	Teaspoon Ground Cloves
⅛	Teaspoon Ground Black Pepper
	Dash Salt

Chai "Cheese" Cake

Cookies and Crème Pound Cake

Statistically speaking, the Oreo® is America's favorite cookie. Yet if forced to share the spotlight with a homemade cake, the choice of which sweet to partake in could be a very tough decision. Luckily, this moist pound cake filled with crunchy cookie pieces makes for an irresistible and delicious compromise in the cookie vs. cake war.

Preheat your oven to 350°F (175°C) and lightly grease a 9 x 5 inch loaf pan.

Using your stand mixer, cream together the margarine and granulated sugar. Add in the flour, baking powder, baking soda, salt, and soy yogurt all at once. Mix until just combined, but be careful not to overwork the batter; a few lumps are okay at this point. Proceed by mixing in the soymilk, followed by the vanilla and vinegar. Fold in your crushed cookies by hand, and pour the batter into your prepared loaf pan. Place the remaining whole cookies on top, and bake for 40 to 50 minutes, until a toothpick inserted into the center of your loaf comes out clean.

Let the cake cool in the pan for at least 5 minutes before unmolding and moving it to a wire rack. Ensure that it is completely cooled before preparing the glaze.

For the glaze, simply whisk together the confectioner's sugar and water, and drizzle liberally over the top of your cake. Slice and enjoy with a tall glass of soymilk, just like the classic cookie!

Makes 10 to 12 Servings

Pound Cake:

¼	Cup Margarine
¾	Cup Granulated Sugar
1	Cup All-Purpose Flour
1	Teaspoon Baking Powder
½	Teaspoon Baking Soda
½	Teaspoon Salt
6	Ounces Unsweetened Soy Yogurt
½	Cup Plain Soymilk
1	Teaspoon Vanilla Extract
½	Teaspoon Apple Cider Vinegar
1	Cup Crushed Vegan Chocolate Crème-Filled Sandwich Cookies (About 10 Whole Cookies)
4	Whole Vegan Chocolate Crème-Filled Sandwich Cookies

Icing:

½	Cup Confectioner's Sugar
2	Teaspoons Water

Cookies and Crème Pound Cake

Decadent Almond Cake

This moist, fine-crumbed cake was originally created for a good friend's birthday celebration, at her request for something featuring almonds and chocolate. Although it looks and tastes incredibly decadent, it is really quite easy to slap together. Covered in a generous coating of chocolate ganache, cake-decorating skills are not required to make this dessert look amazing.

I prefer to grind my own almonds for this recipe, to ensure that there is no grittiness due to roughly ground nuts, but feel free to use a scant cup of almond meal instead if you are short on time!

Preheat your oven to 350°F (175°C) and lightly grease two 8 inch round cake pans.

If using whole almonds, begin by grinding them down into a relatively fine powder with your food processor or blender. If you would like the cake to have a little bit of crunch, then leave the powder a slightly coarse. On the converse side, be careful not to process them for too long, or they will pass the flour stage, releasing their natural oils to turn into nut butter

Transfer the almond flour/meal to a medium bowl and add in the other two flours, baking powder, baking soda, and salt. Stir to combine and set aside.

Using a stand mixer, beat together the oil, soymilk, maple syrup, and vinegar so that the mixture becomes bubbly on the surface. Incorporate the two extracts. Slowly add in the dry mixture, stirring just until everything is combined. Divide the batter between your two prepared pans and bake for 35 to 40 minutes, until a toothpick inserted into the center of each layer comes out clean. Allow the layers to cool for at least 15 minutes before turning them out of the pan. Make sure they are completely cool before decorating.

To make your ganache, heat the chocolate, soy creamer, and maple syrup together in a medium saucepan, and stir thoroughly to create a completely smooth liquid. Pour a fair amount of the ganache over the first layer of your cake before placing the second gently on top of it, being careful not to press the filling out. Pour more ganache over the top of the stack and smooth it down the cake sides. Decorate with sliced almonds if desired. Let the ganache cool and set completely before serving.

Makes 10 to 12 Servings

Almond Cake:

1	Cup Whole Raw Almonds or 1 Scant Cup Almond Meal
1½	Cups All-Purpose Flour
1	Cup Soy Flour
1	Teaspoon Baking Powder
1	Teaspoon Baking Soda
½	Teaspoon Salt
⅔	Cup Canola or Vegetable Oil
2	Cups Plain Soymilk
1¼	Cups Maple Syrup
1	Teaspoon Apple Cider Vinegar
2½	Teaspoons Almond Extract
1	Teaspoon Vanilla Extract

Chocolate Ganache:

14	Ounces Dark Chocolate, Chopped
½	Cup Plain Soy Creamer
¼	Cup Maple Syrup

Sliced Almonds for Garnish
(Optional)

Decadent Almond Cake

Lemon-Lime Sunshine Bundt

Even if you are stuck with nothing but cloudy skies, it is easy to brighten anyone's day with a slice of this cheerful cake. Lemons and limes make me think of bright colors, bubbly sodas, and hot summer days; so using them in a dessert such as this is just like baking sunshine into a cake!

If you are unable to find one of the flavored soy yogurts, simply use an equal amount of unsweetened soy yogurt with 1 additional teaspoon of juice for the missing citrus flavor.

Lemon-Lime Cake:

¾	Cup Plain Soymilk
2	Tablespoons Lemon Juice
2	Tablespoons Lime Juice
1	Cup Margarine
2	Cups Granulated Sugar
1–2	Tablespoons Lemon Zest
1–2	Tablespoons Lime Zest
6	Ounces Lemon Soy Yogurt
6	Ounces Lime Soy Yogurt
3	Cups All-Purpose Flour
2	Teaspoons Baking Powder
½	Teaspoon Salt

Glaze:

½	Cup Confectioner's Sugar
2	Tablespoons Plain Soymilk

Preheat your oven to 325°F (160°C) and lightly grease and flour a 10 inch bundt or tube pan.

In a small bowl, combine the soymilk with both juices and set aside.

In a stand mixer, cream the margarine, sugar, and both zests together until light and fluffy, scraping down the sides as necessary. Add in both containers of soy yogurt, one at a time, beating well after each addition to prevent lumps of margarine from being left behind.

Combine the flour, baking powder, and salt in a separate bowl. Add these dry ingredients into your stand mixer alternately with the citrus soymilk. Mix thoroughly.

Drop dollops of the batter evenly into your prepared bundt pan and bake for 50 to 60 minutes, until a toothpick inserted into the center comes out clean. Let the cake cool in the pan for 10 minutes before turning it out onto a wire rack. Allow it to cool completely before icing.

For the glaze, simply whisk the sugar and soymilk together until smooth, and pour over your cake as desired.

Makes 16 to 18 Servings

Lemon–Lime Sunshine Bundt

Lychee Cupcakes with Raspberry Frosting

Nothing beats fresh fruit, especially if it is baked into sweet little cupcakes. Lychees are not an everyday produce pick, but they are certainly worth hunting down. Fragrant and delicately flavored like flowers or herbs, puréed lychees give these cupcakes an amazing taste. The raspberry frosting goes above and beyond those canned frostings you might find at the store to enhance the flavors locked within each tender, moist crumb. You may wonder how artificial flavors ever found a foothold when the real thing tastes this incredible.

Lychees are one of the more unusual fruits that I have included in my baked goods, but it was simply a serendipitous find when I discovered them at my regular grocery store. They can also be found in most Asian markets, but if you still have no luck in acquiring them, canned lychees will work as well.

Before making any advances toward those cupcake pans, you will want to peel, pit, and process those lychees first. To do so, simply jab your thumb into the top as you would an orange, and remove the outer skin. The fruit itself is a translucent white color; split this in half to remove the pit. Toss the pure flesh into your food processor or blender, and repeat with your remaining lychees. If they are being stubborn, you can always take a knife all the way around them to remove the inedible exterior. Once you have taken care of the lychees, process them until mostly smooth and set aside.

Preheat your oven to 350°F (175°C) and line twelve to thirteen muffin tins with cupcake papers.

In a large bowl, mix together the lychee purée, sugar, oil, and vanilla until completely combined. Next, sift in the flour, baking powder, baking soda, and salt, stirring just enough to bring the batter together, but being careful not to over mix. Finally, once your oven is ready to go, stir in the apple cider vinegar. Spoon the batter into your prepared tins about $1/2$ to $2/3$ of the way to the top. Though you may be able to squeeze the batter into twelve tins, I typically end up with a perfect baker's dozen. Bake for 15 to 17 minutes, until evenly browned and a toothpick inserted into the center of a cupcake, comes out clean. Let the cupcakes cool completely before frosting

For the frosting, cream together the margarine and "cream cheese" in your stand mixer. Make sure you wash and dry your berries well before proceeding. Set aside 13 of the nicest berries for garnish. Throw the rest of the raspberries into your food processor or blender, and blend them until mostly smooth. Pour this purée into your stand mixer, and beat until everything is mostly incorporated. Mix in 2 cups of the confectioner's sugar. Once the first batch of sugar has combined, add the remaining 2 cups. Start mixing on slow, just to incorporate, and then bring the speed up to high, whipping for about 5 minutes until the frosting is light and fluffy. Pipe or spread the frosting onto your cupcakes as desired, and top with the reserved berries.

Makes 13 Cupcakes

Lychee Cupcakes:

3/4	lb Fresh Lychee Nuts (Roughly 7 Ounces of Purée)
3/4	Cup Granulated Sugar
1/3	Cup Canola or Vegetable Oil
1/4	Teaspoon Vanilla Extract
1 1/4	Cups All-Purpose Flour
1/2	Teaspoon Baking Powder
3/4	Teaspoon Baking Soda
1/4	Teaspoon Salt
1/2	Teaspoon Apple Cider Vinegar

Raspberry Frosting:

1/2	Cup Margarine
1/2	Cup Vegan "Cream Cheese"
6	Ounces Fresh Raspberries
4	Cups Confectioner's Sugar

Lychee Cupcakes with Raspberry Frosting

Marshmallow Mud Cake

Just when you thought you had seen it all in terms of chocolate cake, the simple addition of a sinfully sweet marshmallow topping turns it into an entirely different beast. To say that this combination is addictive is a vast understatement, as you may find yourself unable to stop at only one slice, no matter what size you serve. Appealing to both children and adults, this is the easiest crowd-pleaser you might hope to find.

Preheat your oven to 350°F (175°C) and lightly grease a 9 inch round cake pan.

In a microwave-safe bowl, heat the soymilk for about 2 minutes on high so that it just begins to boil. Stir in the cocoa powder, making sure it has completely dissolved before stirring in the vinegar as well. Set aside.

Use your stand mixer to cream together the margarine, both sugars, and the vanilla. Scrape down the sides and add in the oil, beating well to combine. Beat in the cocoa mixture, provided that it has cooled down by now. Sift in the flour, baking soda, and salt, mixing until everything is just incorporated.

Pour the batter into your prepared pan and spread it down into an even layer. Don't worry if it seems like a skimpy amount of batter; it rises a bit in baking, and the marshmallow topping compensates for any lack of height! Bake for 18 to 22 minutes, until a toothpick inserted into the center of the cake, comes out clean. Let it cool completely before removing from the pan and making the topping.

To make the marshmallow topping, begin by combining the shortening, sugar, and vanilla in your stand mixer. Make sure that everything is fully incorporated before adding in half of the Ricemellow Crème. Continue mixing until the topping seems to be fairly homogeneous (it is okay if it looks a little bit curdled), and add in the remaining amount of Ricemellow Crème. Once incorporated, bring the speed of the mixer up to high and whip for about 5 minutes. The resulting mixture should be creamy, silky, and viscous. Spread liberally on top of your cake.

For the final chocolate drizzle, simply melt down the margarine and whisk in the confectioner's sugar, cocoa, and water until smooth. Pour this icing over your cake as desired, or use it as a sauce to serve on the side.

Makes 10 to 12 Servings

Chocolate Cake:

¾	Cup Chocolate Soymilk
½	Cup Dutch Process Cocoa Powder
1	Teaspoon Apple Cider Vinegar
¼	Cup Margarine
¼	Cup Brown Sugar
½	Cup Granulated Sugar
1	Teaspoon Vanilla Extract
2	Tablespoons Canola or Vegetable Oil
1	Cup All-Purpose Flour
1	Teaspoon Baking Soda
¼	Teaspoon Salt

Marshmallow Topping:

½	Cup Vegetable Shortening
3	Cups Confectioner's Sugar
1	Teaspoon Vanilla Extract
1	10-Ounce Container Ricemellow Crème

Chocolate Icing:

1	Tablespoon Margarine
½	Cup Confectioner's Sugar
1	Tablespoon Black Cocoa Powder or Dutch Process Cocoa Powder
1	Tablespoon Water

Marshmallow Mud Cake

Mini Icebox "Cheese" Cake

For myself, sweets are a year round calling, but the hot weather and humidity of summer can be a powerful deterrent to turning on the oven. Fortunately, not all desserts need to be baked, as is the case with this little cake made to beat the heat. Much like an ice cream cake in consistency but with the pleasant tang of cream cheese, it is the best adaptation of a cheesecake under the sun, if I do say so myself. Plus, unlike the large commitment of most cheesecakes, this one is perfectly sized for an intimate party between a few close friends!

Should you prefer a larger cake for a bigger party, double the recipe and use a 10 inch springform pan instead. It will be slightly taller than the small version, but I don't see any problem with bigger slices!

Place the graham cracker crumbs in a medium bowl. Melt the margarine and pour it over the crumbs, along with both syrups. Mix to coat and moisten all of the crumbs, and press the mixture firmly into a 6 inch round springform pan. Press the crust about 1 inch up the sides. Chill it in the freezer while you assemble the filling.

Blend the "cream cheese," sugar, lemon juice, vanilla, and soy creamer in a food processor or blender until the mixture is completely homogeneous. Remove the crust from the freezer, and pour the filling carefully inside. Cover the cake with plastic wrap, and return it to the freezer for at least 3 hours, until firm.

Top with your jam of choice before serving.

Makes 2 to 4 Servings

Graham Cracker Crust:

1	Cup Vegan Graham Cracker Crumbs
3	Tablespoons Margarine
1	Tablespoon Brown Rice Syrup
1	Tablespoon Maple Syrup

"Cheese" Cake Filling:

1	8-Ounce Packages Vegan "Cream Cheese"
1/3	Cup Granulated Sugar
1/2	Teaspoon Lemon Juice
2	Teaspoons Vanilla Extract
1/4	Cup Plain Soy Creamer
1/4	Cup Jam of Your Choice

Mini Icebox "Cheese" Cake

Mocha Devastation Cake

If I were ever to have a "signature" dessert, this would be it. Stealing the top award at my very first baking competition, its success may be to blame for my obsession with creating new and exciting sweet recipes. Intensely flavored with coffee and chocolate, simply leaving this cake uncovered on the counter will draw curious noses in from all over the house to investigate the heavenly aroma. Dense and decadent to say the least, this cake should only be made for a crowd, or else you may find yourself compelled to polish it off unassisted!

Mocha Cake:

2	Cups All-Purpose Flour
½	Cup Dutch Process Cocoa Powder
1	Tablespoon Baking Powder
1	Teaspoon Baking Soda
1	12-Ounce Package Extra-Firm Silken Tofu
1¼	Cups Maple Syrup
1¼	Cups Canola or Vegetable Oil
1	Cup Plain Soymilk
2	Teaspoons Instant Coffee Powder
1	Tablespoon Vanilla Extract

Coffee "Buttercream":

½	Cup Margarine
2	Cups Confectioner's Sugar
1	Tablespoon Vanilla Extract
2	Tablespoons Plain Soy Creamer
2½	Teaspoons Instant Coffee Powder
½	Cup Dark Chocolate-Covered Espresso Beans

Chocolate Coating:

⅔	Cup Plain Soy Creamer
½	Cup Margarine
10	Ounces Dark Chocolate, Chopped
1	Cup Dark Chocolate-Covered Espresso Beans

Preheat your oven to 325°F (160°C) and lightly oil and flour two 8 inch round cake pans.

Sift the flour, cocoa powder, baking powder, and baking soda into your stand mixer and set aside. Drain any excess liquid out of the tofu before tossing it into your food processor or blender, and puréeing it until completely smooth. Scrape down the sides to ensure that no chunks are left behind, and add in the maple syrup and oil, processing just to combine. Add these wet ingredients into the dry ingredients waiting within your mixer. Blend just briefly so that everything becomes a little bit better acquainted.

In a separate microwave-safe bowl, heat the soymilk in the microwave for just a minute and dissolve the coffee powder into it. Add this mixture along with the vanilla into the batter, and stir just enough to fully combine. Divide the resulting batter evenly between your prepared pans. Bake for 30 minutes, until the cakes appear to pull away from the sides slightly. Do not be alarmed if the center collapses in on itself as it cools; this is actually a good thing! Give the layers time to rest and cool off before proceeding.

To make the "buttercream," simply blend all of the ingredients, (except for the espresso beans) in your mixer until smooth and creamy. Crush the ½ cup of espresso beans, and set them aside.

When you are ready to begin assembling the cake, turn the first layer out onto the plate you want to serve it on. In the indentation that formed after the center fell in, mound your "buttercream" up high, using all of it. Sprinkle the crushed espresso beans on top, to evenly cover the entire mountain of filling. Now, take the second layer and flip it right on top of the bottom, so that the indentation encases the filling, resulting in a smooth top.

Finally, heat the soy creamer and margarine together in the microwave for one minute, or until the margarine melts. Place the 10 ounces of dark chocolate in a medium bowl, and pour the margarine mixture over the top. Let it sit for about a minute to heat up and start melting, at which time you should stir vigorously to combine. If it doesn't all smooth out after a good deal of stirring, send it all to the microwave for 30 seconds or so to help it along. Let this smooth ganache sit and thicken for up to an hour at room temperature or for 20 to 30 minutes in the refrigerator. Smooth the ganache over the top of the cake and down the sides. Crush the remaining 1 cup of espresso beans and apply them in an even layer to coat the sides of the cake before the ganache has fully set. Serve this cake within 24 hours to enjoy the flavors and textures at the peak of perfection.

Makes 10 to 12 Servings

Mocha Devastation Cake

Not-Nog Cupcakes

Paging through a Christmas-oriented baking catalog during the holiday season, I found one recipe in particular that held my interest: eggnog bread. As I scanned the ingredients, it occurred to me how incredibly non-vegan this concoction was. The dense loaf was saturated with eggs, milk, butter, and of course eggnog. Converting this into an unlikely vegan variant was a challenge I simply could not turn down! A few failed batches later, the original quick bread was converted into cupcakes, and my kitchen was filled with a veritable army of lightly spiced, sweet holiday gifts. The resulting recipe was made to bring to a large holiday party, so it does make a whole lot of little cakes, but I am sure you won't have any difficulty finishing them off!

Preheat your oven to 350°F (175°C) and line two dozen muffin tins with cupcake papers.

In your stand mixer, cream the margarine with the sugar, nutmeg, vanilla, and salt. Add the soy yogurt and beat thoroughly. While the mixer churns, grind the flax seeds into a powder with a spice grinder, and whiz them together with the water. Introduce the flax mixture into the main bowl and stir to combine. The batter will probably be fairly lumpy at this point, but as long as you do not have any obscenely large clumps of solid margarine, it should be fine.

In a separate vessel, combine your flour, baking powder, and baking soda. Slowly add these dry ingredients to the contents of the bowl waiting in your stand mixer, alternating with the "eggnog" until both are used up. Fully incorporate each addition, but be careful not to over mix.

Pour the resulting batter into your prepared cupcake liners about ⅔ to ¾ of the way full, and bake for 20 to 22 minutes. The cupcakes should not appear browned; so keep a close eye on them. They will be done when a toothpick inserted into the center of a cake comes out clean.

To make the topping, set a saucepan over medium-low heat. Melt the margarine with the brown sugar, corn syrup, and salt, stirring until everything is dissolved and no longer grainy. Once the mixture comes to a boil, reduce the heat and simmer for 10 to 15 minutes, until it has thickened enough to coat the back of a spoon. Remove your pan from the heat and add in the rum, stirring thoroughly. Let the mixture sit for a few minutes before spooning a dollop on top of each cupcake. Top with sliced almonds to cover as desired.

The topping will continue to thicken and firm up slightly as it cools, but it should still remain soft. Serve within 24 hours, or the topping may begin to soak into the cake. It will still be delicious, just a little funny looking!

Makes 24 Cupcakes

Nog Cupcakes:

1½	Cups Margarine
2	Cups Granulated Sugar
1½	Teaspoons Ground Nutmeg
½	Teaspoon Vanilla Extract
1	Teaspoon Salt
6	Ounces Vanilla Soy Yogurt
1	Tablespoon Flax Seeds
2	Tablespoons Water
3¾	Cups All-Purpose Flour
2	Teaspoons Baking Powder
½	Teaspoon Baking Soda
1½	Cups Vegan "Eggnog"

Caramel Topping:

2	Tablespoons Margarine
1	Cup Dark Brown Sugar
½	Cup Light Corn Syrup
¼	Teaspoon Salt
2	Tablespoons Rum (Any Variety)

½–1	Cup Sliced Almonds for Garnish

Not-Nog Cupcakes

Orange Dreamsicle Snack Cake

Turning the creamy combination of orange and vanilla into a moist and easy-to-munch cake is not only a fun new take on the frozen dessert, but an improvement on the original, as you won't need to worry about it melting on you!

Preheat your oven to 350°F (175°C) and lightly grease a 9 x 13 inch baking pan.

Combine the flour, sugar, baking powder, baking soda, and salt in a medium bowl and set aside. In a stand mixer, whisk together the soy yogurt and oil until fully emulsified. Add in the vanilla and orange juice. Slowly incorporate the dry ingredients in stages, until the batter is nicely mixed without lumps. Pour the batter into your prepared pan.

In a small dish, melt the vegetable shortening and whisk in the confectioner's sugar, vanilla, and soy creamer, stirring until smooth. Drizzle over the batter. Microwave the marmalade for about 30 seconds, until slightly liquefied and easier to pour. Drizzle it over the batter as well. Swirl both toppings together with a knife, but try not to overdo it as you may muddle the colors.

Bake for 25 to 30 minutes, until a toothpick inserted into the center of the cake comes out clean. When testing for doneness, be sure to find a spot that is free from topping, as the icing and marmalade may cause the toothpick to appear wet, even if the cake is ready. Wait until the cake has cooled completely before cutting into bars.

Makes 9 to 12 Servings

Snack Cake:

3½	Cups All-Purpose Flour
1½	Cups Granulated Sugar
½	Teaspoon Baking Powder
1	Teaspoon Baking Soda
½	Teaspoon Salt
6	Ounces Vanilla Soy Yogurt
¼	Cup Canola or Vegetable Oil
1	Tablespoon Vanilla Extract
¾	Cup Orange Juice

Dreamsicle Topping:

¼	Cup Vegetable Shortening
1	Cup Confectioner's Sugar
1	Teaspoon Vanilla Extract
2	Tablespoons Plain Soy Creamer
½	Cup Orange Marmalade

Orange Dreamsicle Snack Cake

Peach Melba Layer Cake

As the story goes, the original Peach Melba was created for a famous opera singer who loved ice cream, but did not dare eat it for fear of paralyzing her vocal cords. A brilliant chef thought to pair vanilla ice cream with peaches and a raspberry sauce, so that the added elements might lessen the chill. However, if the chef had really been thinking on his feet, he might have cut the frozen dessert out entirely and made an enticing layer cake topped with a fluffy vanilla frosting. One so smooth and creamy that you would swear it was what warm ice cream would taste like, if only it maintained its composure instead of melting. Hold the ice cream this time, and enjoy a "warm" peach melba.

Preheat your oven to 350°F (175°C) and generously grease and flour two 8 inch round cake pans.

Drain all three cans of peaches thoroughly before tossing the contents into a food processor or blender. Break down the peaches into a mostly smooth purée, but leave a few chunks of fruit to add texture to the cake. Set aside.

In your stand mixer, cream together the margarine and both sugars until light and fluffy. Add in your peach purée along with the vinegar and mix to combine. In a separate bowl, sift together the flours, baking powder, baking soda, and salt. Slowly add these dry ingredients into your stand mixer, and blend until everything is incorporated. Equally divide the batter between your two prepared pans. Bake for 25 to 30 minutes, until a toothpick inserted into the center of each layer comes out clean. Cool completely.

For the vanilla frosting, simply blend all of the frosting ingredients together with a mixer, starting at a low speed so that the sugar does not fly out. Once the ingredients have adequately combined, whip the frosting on a higher speed for at least 3 minutes, to add more air and lighten it a bit.

When you are ready to assemble the cake, turn both layers out of the pans and slice each in half horizontally, to create four round layers total. Use a sawing motion with a serrated knife to achieve a clean cut, and be careful when moving the layers. Place the first bottom layer on the platter you intend to serve it on, and spread it with raspberry jam. To prevent the two fillings from mingling, drop a generous dollop of the vanilla frosting in the very center of the layer (atop the jam) and smooth it down and out to the edges. Put the other unfrosted half of the cake layer on a plate, and flop it neatly on top of the nicely spread filling. Frost the top of this one in the same manner. Repeat the frosting process with the remaining two layers, but skip the raspberry jam on the very top. Simply spread the remaining vanilla frosting and decorate with fresh raspberries, if desired.

Makes 10 to 14 Servings

Peach Cake:

3	15-Ounce Cans Sliced Peaches in 100% Juice (not Syrup)
½	Cup Margarine
1	Cup Granulated Sugar
⅓	Cup Brown Sugar
1	Tablespoon Apple Cider Vinegar
1½	Cups All-Purpose Flour
1	Cup Whole Wheat Pastry Flour
2	Teaspoons Baking Powder
1½	Teaspoons Baking Soda
½	Teaspoon Salt

Vanilla Frosting:

1½	Cups Vegetable Shortening
4	Cups Confectioner's Sugar
¼	Cup Plain or Vanilla Soymilk
1	Tablespoon Vanilla Extract

Raspberry Filling:

1	12-Ounce Jar Raspberry Jam
½	Pint Raspberries for Garnish (Optional)

Peach Melba Layer Cake

Piña Colada Mini-Bundts

Picture yourself lying in the sun, perhaps on some isolated beach in the tropics. Not a worry in the world, you have everything you need, sun block, a good companion, and a refreshing tropical drink. You reach over to take another sip, when you realize that it is not a drink at all, but a tiny cake! In fact, it is then that you realize you are not on the beach, but at home in your kitchen, with a freshly baked batch of these amazing mini-bundts! Even if your environment is cold and gray, you too can have a taste of the sweet life with these unique tropical delights.

Preheat your oven to 350°F (175°C) and lightly grease a mini-bundt pan or a jumbo muffin pan.

Toss 1 cup of the flaked coconut into your food processor, and grind it down into a fine powder consistency. It may take about 5 minutes, but when you see the coconut starting to clump together, it is ready. If you do not have a food processor handy, then whiz the coconut in a spice grinder in batches of ¼ to ½ cup, depending upon the capacity of your appliance.

Place the powdered coconut into your stand mixer along with the margarine and both sugars. Thoroughly cream everything together. Drain any excess liquid from the crushed pineapple, add it to the mixer, and combine. Sift in the flour, baking powder, and salt and mix once more. Stir in the remaining whole flaked coconut, soymilk, rum, and lemon juice, stirring just enough to incorporate everything.

Pour the batter into your prepared mini-bundts and bake for 30 to 35 minutes, until a toothpick inserted into the center of a cake comes out clean. Let the cakes rest in their pans for 10 minutes before transferring them to a wire rack. Allow them to cool completely before icing.

For the glaze, simply whisk the sugar together with as much rum as necessary to achieve a desirable thickness. Drizzle over the bundts, and enjoy a taste of the tropics, from your own home!

Makes 5 Mini-Bundts

Piña Colada Cake:

1½	Cups Unsweetened Flaked Coconut, Divided
¼	Cup Margarine
⅓	Cup Granulated Sugar
2	Tablespoons Brown Sugar
1	Cup Crushed Pineapple, Drained
1	Cup All-Purpose Flour
1	Teaspoon Baking Powder
¼	Teaspoon Salt
¼	Cup Plain Soymilk
2	Tablespoons Dark Rum
1	Teaspoon Lemon Juice

Glaze:

1	Cup Confectioner's Sugar
2–3	Tablespoons Dark Rum

Piña Colada Mini-Bundts

Plum-Good Crumb Cake

Crumb cake is understandably popular around teatime, with just a little spice, a good bit of sugar, and that irresistible topping. In my opinion, the crumb topping is the best part, so this recipe contains an extra-large helping! While this cake is delicious on its own, the addition of fresh plums cements its place at the table with enthusiastic certainty. If plums are not stocked in your fruit basket, try another combination of fresh fruits, such as peaches, apples, or pears. Just adjust the amount of fruit appropriately, as a pear clearly has much more flesh than a wee little plum. No matter what you choose to layer into the center, I am sure you will agree that this moist, sophisticated coffeecake is plum good!

Preheat your oven to 350°F (175°C) and lightly grease a 9 inch angel food cake or tube pan.

For the crumb topping, sift together all of the dry ingredients (flour through salt) in a medium bowl. Melt the margarine and pour it over the flour mixture. Stir with a fork to coat everything evenly, while forming crumbs in various sizes.
Set aside.

Combine the soymilk and vinegar in a medium bowl and whisk together. Let this sit for a few minutes to curdle. Cream the margarine and sugar together in a stand mixer, beating for a few minutes to fully combine. Sift the flour, baking powder, baking soda, and salt into a separate bowl. Add the "sour cream," soy yogurt, and vanilla to your curdled soymilk. Alternately add the dry ingredients with the wet into your mixer, beating on low speed and occasionally scraping down the sides to make sure you do not leave any large lumps behind. Be careful not to over mix, as it is okay to leave a few small lumps in the batter.

Pour half of your batter into the prepared pan, spreading it to coat the bottom in an even layer. Toss the chopped plums with a tablespoon of flour, and sprinkle the fruit over the first layer of batter. Follow this with the remaining half of your batter, being careful to completely cover all of the fruit. Sprinkle all of the reserved crumb mixture over the top, and bake the whole thing for 50 to 55 minutes, until a toothpick or skewer inserted into the center of the cake comes out clean. Let cool completely in the pan prior to serving.

Makes 10 to 12 Servings

Crumb Topping:

1	Cup All-Purpose Flour
½	Cup Dark Brown Sugar
½	Tablespoon Ground Cinnamon
⅛	Teaspoon Ground Cardamom
½	Teaspoon Salt
6	Tablespoons Margarine

Cake:

½	Cup Plain Soymilk
½	Teaspoon Apple Cider Vinegar
½	Cup Margarine
1	Cup Granulated Sugar
2	Cups All-Purpose Flour
1	Teaspoon Baking Powder
1	Teaspoon Baking Soda
½	Teaspoon Salt
¾	Cup Vegan "Sour Cream"
6	Ounces Unsweetened Soy Yogurt
1	Teaspoon Vanilla Extract

Fruit Filling:

3–4	Fresh Plums, Pitted and Chopped
1	Tablespoon All-Purpose Flour

Plumb-Good Crumb Cake

Pomegranate Ginger Cupcakes

Pomegranate may be the food fad of the moment, but this delicious fruit will always have staying power in your home once you try these fragrant cupcakes. With a double dose of juice to intensify the typically delicate flavor, the only thing that could possibly make them better is the sharp but sweet bite of ginger. Much more refined and sophisticated than your average kiddy cupcakes, these will delight the adventurous palate seeking more than just a yellow cake with gaudy rainbow sprinkles.

In a small saucepan over medium heat, cook 1 cup of the juice for about 20 minutes, until it is reduced to a little less than ¼ cup. Remove from the heat and let cool.

Preheat your oven to 350°F (175°C) and line one dozen muffin tins with cupcake papers.

Combine the remaining cup of pomegranate juice and the vinegar in a medium bowl, leaving them alone for a few minutes to get acquainted. Mix the juice vigorously until frothy, and whisk in the sugar, oil, and vanilla. Sift in the flour, baking powder, baking soda, and salt, and stir just until combined. Toss the minced ginger with the remaining 1 tablespoon of flour, and fold both the ginger and zest into your batter.

Divide the batter evenly among the cupcake papers, and drizzle equal amounts of your reserved pomegranate reduction into each cupcake just before baking. Bake for 18 to 22 minutes, until lightly browned, and a toothpick inserted into the center of a cupcake comes out clean. Let the cupcakes cool inside the muffin tins for about 15 minutes, before removing them to a wire rack. Allow them to cool completely before frosting.

In a medium bowl, combine all of the ingredients for the frosting, and whip until smooth and fluffy. Frost your heart out!

Makes 12 Cupcakes

Cupcakes:

2	Cups 100% Pomegranate Juice, Divided
1	Teaspoon Apple Cider Vinegar
¾	Cup Granulated Sugar
⅓	Cup Canola or Vegetable Oil
1	Teaspoon Vanilla Extract
1⅓	Cups + 1 Tablespoon All-Purpose Flour
½	Teaspoon Baking Powder
¾	Teaspoon Baking Soda
¼	Teaspoon Salt
¼	Cup Crystallized Ginger, Finely Minced
½	Tablespoon Lemon Zest

Ginger Frosting:

½	Cup Vegetable Shortening
2	Cups Confectioner's Sugar
1	Teaspoon Vanilla Extract
1	Teaspoon Ground Ginger
2	Tablespoons Plain Soymilk

Pomegranate Ginger Cupcakes

Poppy Seed Cupcakes with Lemon Curd Filling

Whoever discovered that flavors as seemingly mismatched as lemon and poppy seeds could be successfully paired together to make a delicious dessert, was one brilliant lunatic. My only quibble with this combination is that these distinctive components each deserve more time in the spotlight. A crazy concept to be sure, but by sequestering the poppy seeds in the cake and giving the lemon plenty of room to shine in a curd-like filling, each can still be a star of the show.

Lemon "Curd":

½	Cup Instant Mashed Potato Flakes
½	Cup Plain Soymilk
1	Tablespoon Margarine
	Juice (About ¼ Cup) and Zest of 1 Lemon
½	Cup Granulated Sugar

Poppy Seed Vanilla Cupcakes:

1	Cup Plain Soymilk
1	Teaspoon Apple Cider Vinegar
1	Cup All-Purpose Flour
¼	Teaspoon Baking Powder
1	Teaspoon Baking Soda
½	Teaspoon Salt
¼	Cup Canola or Vegetable Oil
½	Cup Granulated Sugar
1½	Tablespoons Poppy Seeds
1	Tablespoon Vanilla Extract

To make the lemon "curd," combine the potato flakes and soymilk in a microwave-safe bowl. Heat them for about 30 seconds so that the starch absorbs all of the liquid. Stir in the margarine, allowing it to melt in the residual heat. Mix in the lemon juice and sugar. Heat the mixture again in the microwave for another 30 to 45 seconds until it reaches a consistency similar to applesauce. Toss it into your food processor or blender along with the lemon zest, and purée for 2 or 3 minutes, until it is completely smooth and creamy. Refrigerate the "curd" for at least 4 hours before using, or better yet, let it sit overnight so that it has time to thicken and intensify in flavor.

With your curd made and chilled, it is time to make the cupcakes! Preheat your oven to 350°F (175°C) and line a dozen muffin tins with cupcake papers.

In a small bowl, whisk together the soymilk and vinegar, and let it rest for 5 minutes. Meanwhile, sift the flour, baking powder, baking soda, and salt into a medium bowl, and set aside. Use your stand mixer to blend the oil and sugar together. Add in your now curdled soymilk and beat the mixture for a minute or two, to form a loose assemblage of bubbles. Slowly add in the dry mix, stirring the batter just enough to combine, being careful not to over mix. Finally, fold in the poppy seeds and vanilla. This makes a very thin, delicate batter; so do not panic if it seems watery.

Pour the batter into your prepared muffin tins, until it reaches about ¾ of the way to the top of the liners. Bake for 17 to 20 minutes, until a toothpick inserted into the center of a cupcake comes out clean. Let the cupcakes cool for 10 minutes in the tins, before removing them to a wire rack, where they should cool completely.

Describing how to assemble the cupcakes can get a bit wordy, so I thought it would be a bit less intimidating to include some step by step photos. (continued on page 118)

Poppy Seed Cupcakes with Lemon Curd Filling

1. First off, get your cupcakes and take the lemon "curd" out of your refrigerator.

2. Take the first cupcake and insert a paring knife at the very edge of the top at an approximately 45-degree angle. Run the blade around the entire circumference at this angle, until the top pops off and you have a little cone of cake.

3. Cut the excess triangle of cake away from the top that you just removed, so that the bottom is smooth. This remaining triangle isn't used for anything else, so go ahead and treat yourself to a snack!

4. Now, take the flat top and press a small, sharp cookie cutter into it. You want to use a shape that leaves a good amount of space around the border so that it doesn't tear. Oh, and you can eat the cutout, too! Who knew this recipe would be so rewarding for the baker?

5. Moving on, take a spoonful of the lemon "curd" and drop it into the hollow in the base of the cake, smoothing it out so that it comes right up to the top.

6. Replace the cupcake top and voila—cupcake art! Just be careful when handling them, because they are a bit more delicate than standard cupcakes.

Makes 12 Cupcakes

Root Beer Float Cupcakes

When I was but a wee tot, and my parents still exercised the authority to regulate my intake of sweets, I remember the harshest restrictions were placed upon soda. It was only once a year, on New Year's Eve that I would be allowed a glass of the bubbly drink. If I was really lucky, I might even get to add a scoop of ice cream and some chocolate syrup to make an ice cream float. These delicious childhood memories were the inspiration for this cup-cake recipe. The root beer flavor is infused into the cake, which is topped with a more grown-up chocolate ganache, and vanilla frosting reminiscent of that cool scoop of ice cream. Playful but still more mature than the original concoction, children and adults alike will be delighted by this twist on a classic dessert!

Preheat your oven to 350°F (175°C) and line a dozen muffin tins with cupcake papers.

In a large bowl, combine the soda and vinegar and let stand for a few minutes. Add in the sugar and oil, whisking vigorously until slightly frothy. Integrate your extracts. In a small bowl, combine the flour, baking powder, baking soda, and salt. Gently introduce this dry mixture into your large bowl, being careful not to over mix.

Distribute the batter evenly between the prepared tins, filling the cupcake liners approximately ¾ of the way to the top. Bake for 18 to 22 minutes, until evenly browned, and a toothpick inserted into the center of a cupcake comes out clean. After letting the cupcakes cool in the pans for about 10 minutes, remove them to a wire rack and allow them to cool completely before preparing the ganache.

When the cupcakes are ready, combine all of the ingredients for the ganache in a microwave-safe container and microwave for about 60 seconds. Stir thoroughly to help incorporate the melting chocolate. If the chocolate is not yet entirely smooth, return the sauce to the microwave for 15 to 30 second intervals, stirring between each heating and watching carefully to ensure that it doesn't burn. Drizzle the ganache in squiggles over the tops of the cupcakes. You will probably have plenty of leftover ganache, but I don't see that as a particularly bad thing. Allow the ganache squiggles to fully cool and dry before preparing the frosting.

With your stand mixer, beat the shortening thoroughly, until creamed. Add in the confectioner's sugar, and beat on a low speed, so as not to spray powder everywhere. Incorporate the soymilk and vanilla, and combine thoroughly, until the frosting is thick and creamy. Apply to your cupcakes and enjoy.

Makes 12 Cupcakes

Root Beer Cupcakes:

1	Cup Root Beer Soda
1	Teaspoon Apple Cider Vinegar
¾	Cup Granulated Sugar
⅓	Cup Canola or Vegetable Oil
½	Teaspoon Vanilla Extract
2	Teaspoons Root Beer Extract
1⅓	Cups All-Purpose Flour
½	Teaspoon Baking Powder
¾	Teaspoon Baking Soda
	Pinch of Salt

Chocolate Ganache:

5	Ounces Dark Chocolate, Chopped
¼	Cup Plain Soymilk
1	Tablespoon Maple Syrup

Vanilla Frosting:

1	Cup Vegetable Shortening
3	Cups Confectioner's Sugar
2	Tablespoons Plain Soymilk
2	Teaspoons Vanilla Extract

Root Beer Float Cupcakes

Self-Frosting Peanut Butter Cupcakes

Okay, you got me, these tasty treats are not going to pick up a knife all on their own, and smear a nice dollop of frosting atop themselves. However, they do come out of the oven fully frosted! The trick is to swirl in a thick spoonful of the peanut buttery cocoa spread before baking them, and presto, your work is all done the instant the timer goes off! Now, if only layer cakes were so self-sufficient...

Preheat your oven to 350°F (175°C) and line one dozen muffin tins with cupcake papers.

In your stand mixer, combine the soymilk and vinegar, and let sit for a few minutes before whisking vigorously until frothy. Mix in both sugars. Grind the flax seeds into a powder with a spice grinder, and whiz them together with the water. Stir the flax seed mixture, peanut butter, applesauce, and vanilla into your mixer, and beat until thoroughly combined. In a separate bowl, add the flour, baking powder, baking soda, and salt. Slowly stir these dry ingredients into the batter. Mix until there are no more lumps, but be careful not to mix more than necessary.

In a separate bowl, combine all of the ingredients for the frosting, and blend until completely smooth. Set aside.

Divide your batter equally between the prepared muffin tins. Drop a dollop of frosting into each cup of raw batter, and swirl it around with a toothpick, covering the entire top. Bake for 20 to 25 minutes, until a toothpick inserted into a cupcake comes out clean. When testing for doneness, be sure to find a spot that is free from frosting, as it may cause the toothpick to appear wet, even if the cupcakes are ready. Let the cupcakes cool inside the tins for at least 10 to 15 minutes. You can either let them cool the rest of the way atop a wire rack, or serve them immediately for a warm delight!

Makes 12 Cupcakes

Peanut Butter Cupcakes:
2/3   Cup Plain Soymilk
1   Teaspoon Apple Cider Vinegar
1/2   Cup Granulated Sugar
1/2   Cup Dark Brown Sugar
2   Tablespoons Flax Seeds
1/4   Cup Water
1/2   Cup Creamy Peanut Butter
1/2   Cup Unsweetened Applesauce
1/2   Teaspoon Vanilla Extract
1 1/2 Cups All-Purpose Flour
1   Teaspoon Baking Powder
1/2   Teaspoon Baking Soda
1/2   Teaspoon Salt

Chocolate Peanut Butter Frosting:
1/2   Cup Creamy Peanut Butter
1/4   Cup Dutch Process Cocoa Powder
2/3   Cup Confectioner's Sugar
1/4   Cup Plain Soymilk

Self-Frosting Peanut Butter Cupcakes

Silken Chocolate Mousse Cake

If love can be equated to chocolate, then consider this cake to be a steamy affair with the seductive temptress next door. Perched atop a soft almond crust is a mousse so rich, smooth and thick that a fork could remain upright in a slice without assistance. Topped off with a scandalous sprinkling of chocolate curls, this little number is hard to resist. Once you have a bit of this creamy, intense indulgence, you may never be able to go back to that plain-Jane chocolate bar.

Lightly grease the bottom of a 9 inch round springform pan.

In a small bowl, combine all of the ingredients for the crust and mix well, until a moist but firm dough forms. Drop the dough into the center of the springform pan, and press it out so that it evenly covers the bottom. It helps if you start by easing the dough out with your fingertips, but to get a nice edge when you reach the sides, simply press the crust in with the bottom of a measuring cup. Once you have the bottom nicely covered, let the crust chill in the refrigerator while you prepare the filling.

Here is where we get to the good part! First, drain any excess liquid away from your tofu before tossing it into your food processor or blender. Purée thoroughly and add in the cocoa, sugar, corn syrup, vanilla, and salt, pulsing briefly to incorporate. Place the chocolate in a microwave-safe dish, and microwave in 30-second intervals to prevent scorching. Stir thoroughly after each heating until the chocolate is completely melted. Continue stirring to achieve a very smooth consistency. Pour the melted chocolate into your waiting tofu mixture. Run the motor for about 2 or 3 minutes; pause to scrape down the sides and process again to achieve a completely smooth, homogeneous mixture.

Pour the filling into your chilled crust, and use a spatula to smooth the top to the best of your ability. The mousse is quite thick and therefore difficult to smooth, but you will be covering up the top with more chocolate anyway! Return your springform pan to the refrigerator, and allow the cake to chill for at least 3 hours.

When you are ready to serve, take a vegetable peeler to your bar of chocolate and shave off thin pieces to adorn the top.

Makes 12 to 16 Servings

Crust:
1½	Cups Almond Meal
⅓	Cup Dutch Process Cocoa Powder
¼	Cup Light Corn Syrup
3	Tablespoons Canola or Vegetable Oil

Chocolate Mousse:
2	12-Ounce Packages Extra-Firm Silken Tofu
½	Cup Dutch Process Cocoa Powder
¾	Cup Granulated Sugar
1	Tablespoons Light Corn Syrup
1	Tablespoon Vanilla Extract
	Pinch Salt
12	Ounces Semi-Sweet Chocolate Chips
1	Bar Dark Chocolate

Silken Chocolate Mousse Cake

Triple Threat Chocolate "Cheese" Cake

Who could resist a cocoa crust topped with three layers of rich "cheese" cake varying in chocolate intensity, and finished off with a simple yet dazzling drizzle of chocolate ganache? If there were ever one dessert to knock your guests off their feet, this would be it. Before I went vegan, I prepared this cake with real cheese and it won a bake-off contest. Now, many years later, I have pulled the recipe back out of the file box and revised it for all to enjoy again. I am happy to say that the delicious taste did not miss a beat in the vegan conversion, either!

Preheat your oven to 350°F (175°C).

For the crust, stir together the graham cracker crumbs, confectioner's sugar, and cocoa in a medium bowl. Melt the margarine and incorporate it into the dry ingredients, forming a crumbly but moist mixture. Use your hands to press this mixture into the bottom of a 9 inch round springform pan. Bring it about ¼ inch further up the sides, to form a lip at the edge of the crust. Set aside.

For the filling, drain the tofu of any excess water and blend it in a food processor or blender until smooth. Add in the vegan "cream cheese", blend, and scrape down the sides. Blend again, ensuring that no lumps remain. Integrate the sugar, vanilla, and salt. Place the 2 cups of chocolate chips in a large microwave-safe bowl, and microwave in 30-second intervals to prevent scorching. Stir thoroughly after each heating until the chocolate is completely melted. Continue stirring to achieve a very smooth consistency.

Remove 1½ cups of the "cheese" mixture and thoroughly blend it into the chocolate. From this mixture, remove 2 cups and spread it evenly atop the crust. Remove 2 additional cups of the "cheese" mixture and blend it into the chocolate mixture. Remove 2 more cups of the resulting mixture and gently spread it over the first chocolate "cheese" cake layer. Finally, stir the rest of the "cheese" filling into the remaining chocolate mixture. Carefully pour and spread this final batch of chocolate mixture over the previous two layers. Work very gently, as the top layers are less solid and more likely to combine. If it happens, don't worry; it will still taste fantastic! Smooth out the top and bake for 50 to 55 minutes. The sides will not pull away from the pan, so you will just have to trust your intuition on this one. After removing it from the oven, use a knife to immediately loosen the cake from the sides, but leave it inside the pan and allow it to cool to room temperature.

Microwave the remaining 2 tablespoons of chocolate chips with the shortening until melted, about 30 to 60 seconds. Stir together and drizzle over top of the cake. Refrigerate the cake for at least 12 hours before serving.

Makes 12 to 16 Servings

Cocoa Crust:

1½	Cups Vegan Graham Cracker Crumbs
⅓	Cup Confectioner's Sugar
¼	Cup Black Cocoa Powder or Dutch Process Cocoa Powder
¼	Cup Margarine

"Cheese" Cake:

1	12-Ounce Package Extra-Firm Silken Tofu
3	8-Ounce Packages Vegan "Cream Cheese"
¾	Cup Granulated Sugar
1	Tablespoon Vanilla Extract
¼	Teaspoon Salt
2	Cups Dark or Semi-Sweet Chocolate Chips

Ganache:

2	Tablespoons Dark or Semi-Sweet Chocolate Chips
½	Teaspoon Vegetable Shortening

Triple Threat Chocolate "Cheese" Cake

Wasabi Chocolate Cupcakes

Don't let their innocent appearance fool you; these are no children's birthday party sweets. Lurking deep within the heart of each tempting chocolate cake is a potent helping of wasabi, surprising even those who are warned of the hidden spice. Wasabi can be extremely powerful even in small quantities, so do not underestimate the meager-looking amounts suggested here, or else you might require a glass or two of soymilk to fight the flames. Spice to your tastes, as some do enjoy the heat more than others, but if you choose to tempt fate and add in more, don't say I didn't warn you!

Preheat your oven to 350°F (175°C) and line one dozen muffin tins with cupcake papers.

Begin by mixing all of the dry ingredients (flour to salt) in a medium bowl. Combine the oil, soymilk, and wasabi in a separate bowl. Beat until the wasabi is fully dissolved and the mixture begins to bubble slightly. Slowly add your wet ingredients to the bowl of dry ingredients and stir until everything is just combined. Be careful not to over mix, as a few lumps are okay. Gently fold in the chocolate chips. Finally, add the vinegar and quickly stir it in.

It may look like more batter than will fit into just one dozen muffin cups, but go ahead and fill the papers most of the way to the top, and immediately slide the tins into the oven. Bake for 18 to 20 minutes, until a toothpick inserted into the center of a cupcake comes out clean. Allow the cupcakes to cool in the tins for at least a few minutes before removing them to a wire rack.

For the icing, whisk the wasabi and soymilk together in a small bowl, ensuring that no lumps of wasabi are left. Add the confectioner's sugar, and whisk until smooth. Drizzle the glaze sparingly over the cupcakes.

Makes 12 Cupcakes

Wasabi Chocolate Cupcakes:

1½	Cups All-Purpose Flour
⅓	Cup Dutch Process Cocoa Powder
1	Cup Granulated Sugar
1	Teaspoon Baking Powder
1	Teaspoon Baking Soda
½	Teaspoon Salt
½	Cup Canola or Vegetable Oil
1	Cup Chocolate Soymilk
1¼–1¾	Teaspoons Wasabi Paste
½	Cup Dark or Semi-Sweet Chocolate Chips, Lightly Tossed in Flour
2	Teaspoons Apple Cider Vinegar

Wasabi Icing:

½	Teaspoon Wasabi Paste
3	Tablespoons Plain Soymilk
1	Cup Confectioner's Sugar

Wasabi Chocolate Cupcakes

PIES & TARTS

Autumn Harvest Pie

What says Fall like crisp apples, tart cranberries, and pure maple syrup? Venture outside of those one-dimensional old recipes that only pay homage to a single aspect of the season, and try something different for Thanksgiving dinner. This recipe always garners raves, as a tiny sliver is enough to convince even die-hard pumpkin pie lovers that other flavors can be fit to grace the table.

Sweet Maple Crust:

2½	Cups All-Purpose Flour
½	Cup Whole Wheat Flour
½	Teaspoon Salt
¾	Cup Margarine, Well-Chilled or Frozen
¼	Cup Maple Syrup
3–5	Tablespoons Plain Soy Creamer

Fruit Filling:

1	Large Apple
½	Teaspoon Lemon Juice
8	Ounces Whole Cranberries, Fresh or Frozen
½	Cup Granulated Sugar
½	Cup Dark Brown Sugar
¼	Cup Cornstarch
¾	Cup Chopped Walnuts
¼	Teaspoon Salt
¼	Teaspoon Ground Nutmeg
2	Tablespoons Margarine

[This step may be done in a food processor] Toss the flours, salt, and margarine into a medium bowl, and combine them with a fork or pastry blender. Continue blending until course crumbs develop and small pieces of margarine are left intact. Mix in the maple syrup, and add the soy creamer one tablespoon at a time, using just enough to bring the dough together into a cohesive ball. You may need to work the dough with your hands as it becomes stiff. Divide the resulting dough into two even pieces, smooth them into round disks, and wrap each tightly with plastic wrap. Refrigerate the dough for at least 2 hours before proceeding.

Once the dough is thoroughly chilled, preheat your oven to 400°F (205°C). Take one of the disks and roll it out to about a ¼ inch thickness on a lightly floured surface. Carefully move the flattened round of dough into a lightly greased 9 inch round pie pan, and patch any holes that may have torn in the transition. Cover the crust loosely with your plastic wrap again, and place the pan in the refrigerator while you assemble the filling.

Peel, core, and chop the apple into bite-sized pieces before tossing it into a large bowl with the lemon juice. Add in all of the remaining ingredients for the filling, except for the margarine, and stir gently to coat the fruit evenly with the dry ingredients. Remove the pie pan from the refrigerator, and pour this fruit and nut mixture into your prepared crust. Cut the margarine into very small pieces, and scatter the chunks atop your filling. Set aside.

Take your second disk of dough and roll it out in a similar fashion, but this time cut out shapes of your choice with a fairly large cookie cutter. Arrange the shapes on top of the filling in a pleasing manner before sliding the whole pie into your oven. Bake for 10 minutes, and then lower the oven temperature to 350°F (175°C) without removing the pie. Bake for an additional 25 to 30 minutes, until the top crust pieces turn golden brown. Let cool for 45 minutes before serving.

Makes 8 to 10 servings

Autumn Harvest Pie

Baklava Tart

Tired of finicky phyllo? Heartbroken over honey? No matter, you can still make a modified baklava that will compete with the best of them. Originally created as a way to use up remnants of phyllo after a little pastry mishap, the phyllo is merely crumbled over the top; so no careful layering is necessary to produce an impressive dessert. The amount of pastry sprinkled on top is very imprecise, allowing a lot of wiggle room to use however much you want. If there aren't any open packages of phyllo dough on hand just waiting to be used up, you can purchase the mini frozen shells and only crush up as many as necessary.

Preheat your oven to 350°F (175°C) and lightly grease a 13 x 4 rectangular tart pan with a removable bottom. While I like how this shape mimics that of a slice of traditional baklava, a 9 inch round fluted tart pan with removable bottom could also be used.

For the crust, cream together the "cream cheese" and both sugars until well combined. Stir in the vanilla, lemon, and agave. Add in 1 cup of the flour, the baking soda, and salt, and mix until fully incorporated. Add the remaining ½ cup of flour, and mix well. Press the resulting mixture into your prepared tart pan, bringing it all the way up the sides. Bake the crust for 15 to 17 minutes, to achieve a light golden brown color. Remove the pan from your oven, but leave the heat on.

In a medium bowl, stir together the walnut pieces, granulated sugar, cinnamon, and salt. Melt the ¼ cup of margarine and pour it over everything inside of the bowl, stirring to coat. Gently press the nut mixture into the crust so that it fits in an even layer. Crumble enough phyllo over the top to cover the nuts completely. Return the pan to the oven, and bake for an additional 20 to 22 minutes, until the phyllo becomes nicely browned.

After removing your tart from the oven, melt the margarine for the glaze in a small bowl. Stir in all of the remaining ingredients and pour this mixture evenly over the top of your tart while it is still warm. This will help bind everything together and sweeten the tart a bit more. Let the tart cool for at least two hours before slicing.

Makes 8 to 14 Servings

Crust:

3½	Ounces Vegan "Cream Cheese"
¼	Cup Granulated Sugar
¼	Cup Dark Brown Sugar
1	Teaspoon Vanilla Extract
½	Teaspoon Lemon Juice
1	Tablespoon Light Agave Nectar
1½	Cups All-Purpose Flour
¼	Teaspoon Baking Soda
¼	Teaspoon Salt

Nutty Filling:

2	Cups Chopped Walnuts
⅓	Cup Granulated Sugar
1	Tablespoon Ground Cinnamon
	Pinch Salt
¼	Cup Margarine
	Phyllo Dough Scraps (About ¼ of a Package, or 8–10 Frozen Mini Shells)

Glaze:

2	Tablespoons Margarine
⅓	Cup Light Agave Nectar
1	Tablespoon Dark Brown Sugar
½	Teaspoon Ground Cinnamon
½	Teaspoon Lemon Juice
½	Teaspoon Vanilla Extract

Baklava Tart

Cashew Crème Pear Tart

Imagine delicately spiced pears cooked just until fork tender, sitting atop a luscious pillow of maple-scented cashew crème, all contained within a soft, nutty crust. Sound like a dream? Well wake up, because this delight is easily a reality! This is one amazing finish to any meal, sure to please all palates and diets alike. Not only is it gluten-free, but this tart can also be adapted for a low-sugar dessert. Simply omit the granulated sugar in the pear topping, and replace the granulated sugar in the crust with more almond meal. Just be sure to save yourself a generous slice beforehand, as the likelihood of leftovers by the end of the night will be slim to none!

In sticking with the gluten-free theme, this tart utilizes brown rice flour for a wonderfully textured crust. Brown rice flour can be found among the other specialty flours in the baking aisle, and in some bulk food departments. Though nutritionally inferior, white rice flour can be substituted measure for measure should the brown rice version be difficult to find.

Preheat your oven to 325°F (160°C).

Combine the sugar, almond meal, and brown rice flour in a medium bowl. Melt the margarine and pour it in, along with the brown rice syrup. Stir to coat all of the dry ingredients thoroughly, and press this mixture firmly into the bottom of a 9 inch round springform pan. Bring the crust about 1 inch up the sides of the pan, and set aside.

If using whole cashews, begin by grinding them down in your food processor. It may take 5 to 10 minutes for the cashews to begin releasing their natural oils and turn into a smooth paste, but don't stop short, as it is important that there are no lumps. Add your freshly processed cashew butter, or a store bought version (available in many natural food stores), to your blender or food processor along with the water, maple syrup, and vanilla. Process to combine. Smooth the resulting crème into your crust and set aside again.

To core and slice your pears, cut them in half lengthwise, and then cut each half into slices of about ⅛ inch thickness. There is no need to peel the pears, as the skins add extra flavor, texture, and fiber. Toss the slices with the sugar and cinnamon, and arrange them on top of your cashew crème. Bake for 20 to 25 minutes, until the pears soften. Let cool and sprinkle with sliced almonds before serving.

Makes 12 to 14 Servings

Crust:

⅓	Cup Granulated Sugar
1	Cup Almond Meal
¼	Cup Brown Rice Flour
¼	Cup Margarine
2	Tablespoons Brown Rice Syrup

Cashew Crème:

1½	Cups Whole, Raw Cashews or 1 Cup Cashew Butter
⅓	Cup Water
¼	Cup Maple Syrup
1	Teaspoon Vanilla Extract

Pear Topping:

2	Firm, Medium-Sized Pears
¼	Cup Granulated Sugar
½	Teaspoon Ground Cinnamon
¼	Cup Sliced Almonds for Garnish

Cashew Crème Pear Tart

Chocolate Chip Cookie Pie

Borrowing from the best aspects of the classic chocolate chip cookie, this pie has the perfect hint of vanilla, the indulgence of caramelized brown sugar, and just the right amount of chocolate. Soft and gooey straight out of the oven, it is like childhood memories all stuffed into a tender crust. Serve this dessert with something light, like fruit or vegan whipped "cream", as it can be quite rich on its own.

Crust:

¼	Cup Margarine
4½	Ounces Vegan "Cream Cheese"
1⅓	Cups All-Purpose Flour
¼	Teaspoon Salt
¼	Teaspoon Baking Powder
1½	Teaspoons Apple Cider Vinegar
2	Tablespoons Plain Soymilk

Cookie Dough Filling:

2	Tablespoons Flax Seeds
1	Cup All-Purpose Flour
½	Cup Granulated Sugar
½	Cup Dark Brown Sugar
10	Tablespoons Margarine
1	Teaspoon Vanilla Extract
¼	Teaspoon Salt
8	Ounces Semi-Sweet Chocolate Chips

[This step may be done in a food processor] For the crust, combine the margarine, "cream cheese," and flour in a medium bowl, using a fork or pastry blender. The mixture should reach a consistency similar to coarse crumbs. Being careful not to overwork the dough, mix in the salt, baking powder, and vinegar. Slowly drizzle in the soymilk while continuing to stir; add in just enough to bring the dough together into a solid lump when squeezed. Turn the dough out onto a flat surface, pressing it together into one cohesive ball with your hands. Wrap it in plastic wrap and refrigerate for at least one hour.

Once chilled, roll the dough out onto a well-floured surface, forming a circle that is approximately 12 inches in diameter. Gently move the circle into a 9 inch round pie pan, and flute the edges as desired. Loosely cover the crust in plastic wrap, and return it to your refrigerator while you assemble the filling.

Preheat your oven to 325°F (160°C).

For the filling, grind the flax seeds into a fine powder, and add it to a large bowl, along with the flour and both sugars. Melt the margarine and stir it into your dry ingredients. Follow with the vanilla, salt, and chocolate chips, stirring thoroughly to combine. This mixture will be very thick, just like your standard cookie dough.

Remove your crust from the refrigerator, and press the cookie dough filling evenly into it with a spatula. Bake for 55 to 60 minutes, until the center appears to have puffed up a bit and the crust is golden brown. Let the pie cool for about 30 minutes. If you let it cool all the way down to room temperature, reheat individual slices in the microwave and serve warm.

Makes 8 to 10 Servings

Chocolate Chip Cookie Pie

Coconut Custard Pie

If you are a fan of coconut, then this pie is for you! Intensely flavored but without overwhelming the taste buds, the creamy coconut custard alone will make you swoon. In fact, should you find yourself pressed for time, just skip the crust altogether and chill the filling in individual custard dishes for a simple tropical treat.

Crust:

1	Cup All-Purpose Flour
1	Tablespoon Sugar
¼	Teaspoon Salt
½	Cup Vegetable Shortening
¼	Cup Cold Water

Coconut Custard:

6	Ounces Extra-Firm Silken Tofu (½ Package)
1	Cup Regular Coconut Milk
1	Cup Granulated Sugar
¼	Cup Margarine
2	Tablespoons All-Purpose Flour
1	Teaspoon Vanilla Extract
1½	Cups Unsweetened Flaked Coconut
¼	Cup Unsweetened Flaked Coconut for Garnish, Toasted

In a medium bowl, combine the flour, sugar, and salt. Add the shortening and work it through with a fork or pastry cutter until the mixture resembles coarse crumbs. Add the water and continue working it gently with your hands until it comes together into a ball of dough. Cover the dough with plastic wrap, and refrigerate until chilled, at least 30 minutes.

Remove the dough from the refrigerator and roll it out onto a lightly floured surface. Aim for a circular shape that is 1 to 1½ inches larger than your pie tin, and about ⅛ inch thick. Very gently fold the circle in half and then in half again, so that you can lift it without tearing, and carefully unfold it into a 9 inch round pie pan. Cover any tears that might have occurred, and flute the edges as desired. Set aside.

Preheat your oven to 350°F (175°C).

Using a food processor or blender, purée the tofu until completely smooth. Add in the coconut milk and sugar, processing to combine. Melt the margarine, and mix it in along with the flour and vanilla. Fold in the coconut by hand, and pour this mixture into your crust.

Bake for 40 to 50 minutes, until the crust is nicely browned and the filling appears to have risen a bit. The pie will still be wobbly in the center, but it will continue to set up as it cools. Let the pie sit for at least an hour before sprinkling the toasted coconut on top and serving.

Makes 8 to 10 Servings

Coconut Custard Pie

Ginger Dream Pie

Why choose a bland vanilla cream pie when you can treat your taste buds to the bright flavors of ginger instead? My passion for the sub-tropical, sweet spice is obvious throughout this creamy concoction. Using a triple dose of ginger that is candied, dried, and fresh, this pie offers a tantalizing combination of hot and cold that still manages to taste refreshing thanks to a quick chill in the refrigerator.

Preheat your oven to 350°F (175°C) and lightly grease and flour a 10 inch round springform pan.

In a medium bowl, cream together the margarine and sugar until soft and fluffy. Ensure that the crystallized ginger is very finely minced, with no large chunks, as it can become overwhelming. Adjusting the amount (¼ to ½ cup) to the sensitivity of your palate, add the crystallized ginger to your bowl along with the almond meal, flour, ground ginger, and lemon juice. Stir so that the mixture is thoroughly combined, but still somewhat crumbly. Press this into the bottom of your prepared pan and bake for 13 to 16 minutes, until it just begins to brown around the edges.

For the filling, begin by draining any excess water from the tofu. Add the tofu to your food processor or blender, and process it until smooth. In a small bowl, combine the sugar, baking powder, salt, and both gingers. Add this sugar mixture to the puréed tofu, and process again. With the motor running, slowly sprinkle in the cornstarch to prevent lumps from forming. Continue processing until everything is fully incorporated. Finally, mix in the vanilla. Pour this mixture into your prepared crust, smoothing the top with a spatula. Bake for 20 to 24 minutes, until the edges appear to have pulled away from the pan slightly. The center may still be wobbly when it comes out of the oven, but it will continue to set as it cools.

Chill the pie thoroughly (at least 2 hours) before serving, and sprinkle with additional confectioner's sugar if desired.

Makes 12 to 14 Servings

Ginger Crust:

½	Cup Margarine
⅓	Cup Granulated Sugar
¼–½	Cup Crystallized Ginger, Finely Minced
⅓	Cup Almond Meal
1	Cup Whole Wheat Pastry Flour
1	Teaspoon Ground Ginger
1	Teaspoon Lemon Juice

Ginger "Cream" Filling:

2	12-Ounce Packages Firm Silken Tofu
1½	Cups Confectioner's Sugar
1	Teaspoon Baking Powder
¼	Teaspoon Salt
1	Tablespoon Ground Ginger
½	Tablespoon Fresh Grated Ginger
2	Tablespoons Cornstarch
2	Tablespoons Vanilla Extract

Ginger Dream Pie

Mexican Chocolate Tart

Although it is fairly simple to make and effortless to dress up, a single bite will reveal that this is no ordinary chocolate tart. With a kick of spice and the crunch of pecans, the myriad of flavors and textures will entertain your palate well beyond an average chocolate dessert. Try serving this rich but modestly sweetened tart with a dollop of vegan whipped "cream" or vanilla "ice cream" to contrast the intense and spicy flavors.

Candied Pecans:

2	Tablespoons Granulated Sugar
1	Tablespoon Dark Brown Sugar
1½	Cups Pecan Halves
1	Teaspoon Ground Cinnamon
¼	Teaspoon Ground Cayenne Pepper
¼	Teaspoon Salt
1	Tablespoon Margarine

Chocolate Crust:

1½	Cups Chocolate Wafer Cookie Crumbs
¼	Cup Granulated Sugar
1	Teaspoon Ground Cinnamon
¼	Teaspoon Salt
½	Cup Margarine

Chocolate Filling:

8	Ounces Dark Chocolate, Broken Into Pieces
½	Teaspoon Ground Cinnamon
¼–½	Teaspoon Ground Cayenne Pepper
1	Cup Plain Soy Creamer
¼	Cup Margarine
¼	Teaspoon Almond Extract
1	Teaspoon Vanilla Extract

Preheat your oven to 350°F (175°C) and line a baking sheet with a silpat or parchment paper.

In a medium bowl, toss together the sugars, pecans, cinnamon, cayenne, and salt. Melt the margarine and pour it over these ingredients, tossing the nuts so that they are evenly coated. Spread the pecans in one even layer on your prepared baking sheet. Bake for about 15 minutes, but be very careful not to cook them for too long. By the time the pecans start to look dark brown or smell nutty, they are probably already burnt. Once removed from the oven, immediately transfer the pecans to a fresh sheet of parchment paper, shake off any excess glaze, and separate any that are touching one another. Let the pecans cool, but leave the oven on.

For the crust, combine the cookie crumbs, sugar, cinnamon, and salt in a medium bowl. Melt the margarine and pour it in, stirring to form a moist but crumbly mixture. Press this into a 9 inch round springform pan or tart pan with a removable bottom. Bring the crust about an inch up the sides of the pan. Bake for 20 minutes and set aside.

To make the filling, place the chocolate pieces, cinnamon, and cayenne in a large bowl. Separately, begin heating the soy creamer in a small saucepan over medium heat. Add the margarine into the saucepan, one tablespoon at a time until each piece melts. Bring it just to a boil, then immediately pour it into the bowl containing your chocolate. Let everything sit for a couple of minutes, and then stir vigorously to melt the chocolate and form a completely smooth mixture. As the chocolate cools, add in both extracts. Pour the chocolate mixture into your prepared crust, and tap lightly on the counter to remove any air bubbles. Let it sit for 15 minutes before placing your glazed pecans around the perimeter. Chill the tart in the refrigerator for 3 hours, and let it sit at room temperature for about 10 to 15 minutes before serving.

Makes 12 to 14 Servings

Mexican Chocolate Tart

Mont Blanc Tart

Let's be honest, a real Mont Blanc is quite different from my interpretation. While the original begins with a base of meringue instead of a crust, this version is much easier to prepare and just as delicious. Concealing a smooth maple crème filling with a generous mound of sweet chestnut crème, it is perfect for the serious sweet tooth. Even if it's not a very authentic rendition of the dessert first created in honor of a mountain in the Alps, it still makes for one fantastic tart.

Almond Crust:

¾	Cup Almond Meal
½	Cup All-Purpose Flour
2	Tablespoons Granulated Sugar
¼	Teaspoon Salt
⅓	Cup Margarine
2	Tablespoons Vegan "Sour Cream"
½	Teaspoon Almond Extract

Maple Crème Filling:

⅓	Cup Whole, Raw Cashews or 3 Tablespoons Cashew Butter
6	Ounces Extra-Firm Silken Tofu (½ package)
¼	Cup Maple Syrup
1½	Teaspoons Vanilla Extract

Chestnut Crème:

15	Ounces Whole, Roasted Chestnuts
2	Tablespoons Plain Soy Creamer
4	Cups Confectioner's Sugar
1	Teaspoon Vanilla Extract
	Powdered Sugar for Topping (Optional)

Preheat your oven to 350°F (175°C).

In a medium bowl, stir together the almond meal, flour, sugar, and salt. Cut the margarine in with a pastry cutter or your fingers, until the mixture resembles coarse crumbs. Mix in the "sour cream" and almond extract, making sure to thoroughly distribute all of the ingredients. You should end up with a relatively homogeneous and cohesive dough. At this point, turn the dough out onto a lightly floured surface and roll it into a circular shape that is about ⅛ inch thick. If it gives you grief, chill the dough for 30 minutes to make it more compliant. Lay the circle inside a 6 inch round springform pan, or sturdy paper liner like I used. Press the dough gently with your fingers to smoothly fill the edges and corners without tearing.

Bake the crust for 13 to 14 minutes before checking on it. It's not unusual for this type of crust to begin sagging at this time, so if you catch it slacking, take this opportunity to carefully reform the crust and fix any gaps, keeping in mind that it is still very hot! Lower the oven to 325°F (160°C), and bake the crust for an additional 5 to 8 minutes, until it browns lightly. Let it cool completely while you assemble the fillings.

If using whole cashews, begin grinding them down in your food processor. It may take 5 to 10 minutes for the cashews to begin releasing their natural oils and turn into a smooth paste, but don't stop short, as it is important that there are no lumps. Drain any excess water away from the tofu and combine it with your freshly processed or store bought cashew butter (available in many natural food stores) in your food processor or blender. Blend until the tofu is completely puréed and incorporated into the cashew paste. Add the maple syrup and vanilla, blending to combine, and smooth the resulting mixture into your crust.

After thoroughly washing all parts of your food processor or blender, reassemble it to grind down the chestnuts. Process the chestnuts until completely smooth. Add in the soy creamer and half of the confectioner's sugar, blending until everything is fully combined. Add in the remainder of the sugar as well as the vanilla and mix thoroughly. Transfer this mixture into a pastry bag fitted with an angel hair tip. Pipe the chestnut crème on top of the maple crème layer in a circular path. Dust with confectioner's sugar if desired.

Makes 4 to 8 Petite Servings

Mont Blanc Tart

Pink Lemonade Tartlets

Just like the brilliant pink glasses of chilly lemonade that you might find at any picnic or backyard barbecue, these two-bite treats offer a refreshingly tart taste of citrus, tempered by a light sweetness. However, these hand-held lemonade delights do have a leg up on the competition, as they derive their rosy coloring from nothing more exotic than raspberry jam, as opposed to the mysterious chemicals found in commercial drink mixes. Eating seasonally does have its benefits, but these ingredients can easily be obtained all year round, so there is no reason not to enjoy a taste of summer any day!

Preheat your oven to 350°F (175°C) and lightly grease two mini-muffin pans.

For the crust, begin by beating the margarine and sugar in your stand mixer until light and creamy. Grind the flax seeds into a powder with a spice grinder, and whiz them together with the water. Add the flax mixture into your mixer and blend well. Add half of the flour, mixing until it is completely incorporated. Follow with the other half of the flour along with the salt, and mix until smooth. If the dough is still crumbly, add up to 2 additional tablespoons of water, just so the mixture sticks together. Drop walnut-sized balls of dough into each prepared muffin tin and press the dough up the sides of the pan using your fingers or the end of a wooden spoon, to form the tartlet shells. Bake for 12 to 15 minutes, until lightly browned. Let the tartlet shells cool completely.

To make the filling, heat the soymilk in a saucepan over medium heat. As the temperature begins to rise, add in the cornstarch and whisk vigorously to prevent lumps from forming. Continue stirring, and in 2 to 4 minutes of even heating, the mixture should thicken significantly. Add the jam and sugar, stirring to dissolve. Remove the mixture from the heat and whisk in the lemon juice. Spoon your pink lemonade filling into the tartlet shells and chill for at least an hour before serving. Garnish the tartlets with fresh raspberries if desired.

Makes 24 Tartlets

Crust:
6	Tablespoons Margarine
½	Cup Confectioner's Sugar
1	Tablespoon Flax Seed
2	Tablespoons Water
1½	Cups All-Purpose Flour
¼	Teaspoon Salt

Lemon Custard:
1	Cup Plain Soymilk
2	Tablespoons Cornstarch
2	Teaspoons Raspberry Jam
⅓	Cup Confectioner's Sugar
2	Tablespoons Lemon Juice
½	Pint Raspberries for Garnish (Optional)

Pink Lemonade Tartlets

Pumpkin Pecan Pie

At last, a delicious resolution to the pumpkin vs. pecan pie battle. While I had never felt that either pie was worthy of all the hype, it appears they simply needed to be combined in order to achieve their full potential. A pure pumpkin pie struck me as monotonous in texture and flavor, while standard pecan pies were always tooth-achingly sweet. However, when I brought them together in one crust, the two fillings seemed to accentuate one another. The pecans do have a more dominant presence, but a dollop of pumpkin crème topping allows both flavors to have an equal turn in the spotlight. Who says you can't make everyone happy?

Crust:
1½	Cups Whole Wheat Pastry Flour
2	Tablespoons Granulated Sugar
½	Teaspoon Salt
½	Cup Margarine
2	Tablespoons Plain Soy Creamer

Pumpkin Filling:
1	Cup Pumpkin Purée
⅓	Cup Granulated Sugar
2	Tablespoons Plain Soy Creamer
½	Teaspoon Ground Cinnamon
¼	Teaspoon Ground Nutmeg
¼	Teaspoon Ground Ginger
2	Tablespoons Cornstarch

Pecan Filling:
1	Cup Pecan Halves
⅓	Cup Light Corn Syrup
⅓	Cup Maple Syrup
¼	Cup Dark Brown Sugar
½	Teaspoon Vanilla Extract

Pumpkin Crème:
6	Ounces Firm Silken Tofu (½ Package)
½	Cup Pumpkin Purée
2¼	Cups Confectioner's Sugar
½	Teaspoon Ground Cinnamon
½	Cup Cornstarch
2	Tablespoons Arrowroot Powder

Preheat your oven to 350°F (175°C) and lightly grease a 9 inch round pie pan.

To begin forming the crust, combine the flour, sugar, and salt in a medium bowl. Melt the margarine and pour it over the dry ingredients. Follow with the soy creamer, and mix until everything comes together into a cohesive dough. Move the dough into your prepared pie pan and press it gently into the bottom and up the sides using the palm of your hand. Flute the edges if desired. Let the crust chill in the refrigerator while you assemble the filling.

In your stand mixer, combine the pumpkin purée, granulated sugar, soy creamer, and spices. Slowly sprinkle in the cornstarch while running the mixer, to prevent lumps. Smooth this filling into your chilled crust, and return the pie pan to the refrigerator.

In a separate bowl, toss the pecans with the corn syrup, maple syrup, brown sugar, and vanilla. Gently and evenly pour this pecan mixture over your pumpkin filling. Don't worry if it looks like a skimpy amount; It will rise to the occasion once completed.

Bake the pie for approximately 25 minutes, until the crust just begins to brown. Lower the oven temperature to 300°F (150°C) and bake the pie for an additional 5 to 8 minutes, making sure that all of the exposed crust looks fully cooked and nicely browned. If it is darkening too quickly, cover the edges with a strip of aluminum foil to prevent burning. Let cool completely.

To make the pumpkin crème, blend the tofu in a food processor or blender until it is completely smooth. Add in the pumpkin, sugar, and cinnamon, processing again to combine. Slowly sprinkle in the cornstarch and arrowroot with the motor running. If it is still too soft to pipe around the border, let this mixture sit in the refrigerator for a few minutes to chill and solidify. Pipe or drop dollops of the crème around the edge of your pie before serving.

Makes 8 to 10 Servings

Pumpkin Pecan Pie

MISCELLANEOUS MORSELS

AND DESSERTS

Brilliant Berry Parfaits

With a stunning visual presentation and a luscious flavor to match, these elegant parfaits will impress both vegans and omnivores alike. Plus, they are easily prepared beforehand, waiting in the refrigerator and ready when you are. Light, sweet, and refreshing, I certainly wouldn't pass up this quick and delicious fix after a long day in the sun.

Blueberry Mousse:

16	Ounces Fresh or Frozen Blueberries
1	12-Ounce Package Extra-Firm Silken Tofu
1	Tablespoon Lemon Juice
2/3	Cup Granulated Sugar
2	Tablespoons Arrowroot Powder
1	Tablespoon Powdered Agar
2	Tablespoons Water

Maple Crème:

1	12-Ounce Package Firm Silken Tofu
1/4	Cup Maple Syrup
1	Tablespoon Vanilla Extract
1/3	Cup All-Purpose Flour

Strawberries for Garnish (Optional)

If frozen, let the blueberries sit at room temperature to thaw completely. Drain the tofu and purée it in your food processor or blender until completely smooth. Drain any excess liquid from the berries before tossing them in with the tofu. Blend the two ingredients for 3 to 4 minutes, to fully combine them and achieve a smooth texture. Add in the lemon juice, sugar, and arrowroot, and process just to mix them in. In a small dish, heat the agar with the water for 15 to 30 seconds in the microwave, just long enough to dissolve the agar and form a gluey, translucent jelly. Don't drag your feet at this stage: quickly, get the agar mixture into your food processor or blender with the other ingredients, and run the motor immediately or the agar will solidify and create gummy lumps that will not dissolve. Once everything is completely mixed in, spoon the mousse into any clear glasses that you wish to serve it in. Let the mousse sit in the refrigerator for at least 2 hours to set up.

After thoroughly cleaning your food processor or blender, process your second package of tofu into a completely smooth, silky purée. Incorporate the maple syrup, vanilla, and flour and process just enough to mix. Chill this mixture for at least 30 minutes before piping or spooning a dollop on top of your blueberry mousse. Top with fresh strawberries right before serving, if desired.

Makes 6 to 8 Servings

Brilliant Berry Parfaits

Cherry Chocolate Truffles

Something that sounds so sinful must be bad for you, right? Unbelievable but true, these sweet morsels need absolutely no added sugar to taste positively decadent. Although few desserts truly qualify as "health food," both the fruit and chocolate could be considered antioxidant-rich foods, allowing you to enjoy these truffles with a clear conscience!

Cherry Center:
1½ Cups Dried Cherries
½ Cup Dutch Process Cocoa Powder

Chocolate Coating:
4 Ounces Dark Chocolate,
    Chopped
2–3 Tablespoons Plain Soy Creamer

Purée the cherries in your food processor until they become a smooth paste. Add in the cocoa and process again. Continue blending and soon enough the whole mixture should come together into a firm ball. Move this dough to a storage container on the counter and allow the flavors to develop overnight. You can continue working with the dough, if you are in a hurry, but I highly suggest you give it time to rest.

Once the dough is ready, scoop a small amount and roll it into a ball in the palm of your hands. The size of each ball will dictate the final size of each truffle. I would suggest about 1 tablespoon of dough for the core, but you may choose to go larger or smaller. Repeat this process until the entire fruit base is used up.

Once you have the cherry centers ready to go, place the chocolate in a small, microwave-safe bowl. Melt the chocolate in the microwave in 30-second intervals, just until it stirs together smoothly with no lumps. Stir in the soy creamer to your desired consistency. More soy creamer will result in a higher ratio of center to coating and the coating will be softer, while less will give you a thicker chocolate shell that solidifies more. Drop one cherry center into the chocolate at a time, rolling it around to completely coat. Once fully coated, drop each truffle onto a piece of parchment paper. At room temperature, allow at least two hours of drying time. However, you can always stash the truffles in your refrigerator or freezer to speed up the process.

Makes Approximately 24 Truffles

Cherry Chocolate Truffles

Cocoa Crumble

Warm and gooey, yet in no way photogenic or sophisticated, crumbles are the very definition of comfort food in my book. Feel free to switch out the fruits depending on what you have on hand. Even if you only have canned fruits that are presweetened, go ahead and toss them in, just leave out the additional sugar in the fruit base. This family-style dessert is so easy to make that even the most inexperienced baker can pull it off in a snap.

Preheat your oven to 375°F (190°C).

For the crumble, cream together the margarine and both sugars using a stand mixer. Add in the cocoa powder, followed by the flour, rolled oats, and salt. Keep mixing until most of it comes together in loose crumbs of varying sizes. Set aside.

Wash and hull the strawberries, and chop them into bite-sized pieces. Drain the cherries and combine them with the strawberries in a large bowl. Toss this fruit with the cornstarch and sugar, and transfer the entire mixture into a 2 quart casserole dish. Spread the berries in as smooth a layer as possible. Sprinkle the prepared crumb topping evenly over the entire surface. Bake for 45 to 50 minutes, until the juices bubble up around the edges. Let the crumble cool for at least 10 minutes before serving.

For the fullest flavor, make this a day ahead, and allow the various ingredients to "marry" in the refrigerator overnight. Simply heat the crumble in a 350°F (175°C) oven for 5 to 10 minutes to warm through before serving. For the ultimate home-style treat, top each serving with a scoop of dairy-free vanilla "ice cream."

Makes 10 to 12 Servings

Crumble:

½	Cup Margarine
½	Cup Dark Brown Sugar
¼	Cup Granulated Sugar
¼	Cup Dutch Process Cocoa Powder
¾	Cup All-Purpose Flour
½	Cup Rolled Oats
¼	Teaspoon Salt

Fruit Base:

2	16-Ounce Containers Fresh Strawberries
1	24-Ounce Jar Unsweetened Pitted Cherries, Drained
2	Tablespoons Cornstarch
⅔	Cup Granulated Sugar

Cocoa Crumble

Five-Minute Coconut Fudge

Rich, thick, and creamy, this fudge is the real stuff. Even the smallest squares will satisfy the most dedicated chocoholics. Plus, it takes mere minutes to whip up, for an instantly gratifying, and heavenly, chocolate treat.

1	Cup Semi-Sweet Chocolate Chips
3½	Cups Confectioner's Sugar
½	Cup Dutch Process Cocoa Powder
2	Tablespoons Margarine
½	Cup Regular Coconut Milk
½	Teaspoon Vanilla Extract
1	Cup Unsweetened Flaked Coconut, Toasted

Lightly grease an 8 x 8 inch square baking pan.

In a large bowl, combine the chocolate chips, sugar, and cocoa. Separately, place the margarine and coconut milk in a small saucepan, and stir together over medium heat. Cook the mixture until the margarine has melted, and bubbles just begin to break at the surface. Remove it from the stove, and immediately pour over the chocolate mixture. Let everything sit for a couple of minutes, and then stir vigorously to melt the chocolate and incorporate the dry ingredients. Continue stirring until a completely smooth mixture forms. Mix in the vanilla, and quickly pour everything into your prepared pan. Smooth out the top and sprinkle the flaked coconut evenly over the entire exposed surface. Press the coconut gently into the fudge with the palm of your hand. Let cool completely before cutting into squares.

Makes 32 Small Squares

Five-Minute Coconut Fudge

Flaming Hot Peanut Brittle

Packed with some serious heat, this nutty candy is well suited to spice-lovers. Be sure to warn your friends before they dig in, as I have witnessed a couple of alarming reactions from those with less adventurous taste buds. This brittle can have some serious after-burn, so it might be good to have a tall glass of soymilk on hand to tame the fire!

1	Cup Roasted, Salted Peanuts
¼	Teaspoon Ground Cayenne Pepper
¼	Teaspoon Ground Paprika
¼	Teaspoon Ground Cinnamon
½	Teaspoon Ground Chili Powder
⅛	Teaspoon Freshly Ground Black Pepper
1¼	Cups Granulated Sugar
¼	Cup Water
¼	Cup Light Corn Syrup
½	Teaspoon Baking Soda

Lay a silpat or generous length of parchment paper on a flat working space near your stove.

Toss the peanuts and spices together in a small bowl and set aside.

Heat the sugar, water, and corn syrup together in a saucepan over medium heat, stirring until the sugar dissolves and the whole mixture comes to a steady boil. Stir continuously while cooking for another 5 to 8 minutes, until your mixture thickens and becomes light amber in color. If you have a candy thermometer handy, the temperature should be somewhere in the neighborhood of 350°F (175°C).

Quickly stir in the reserved peanuts and spices, coating all of the nuts without burning them. Add the baking soda, remove the pan from the heat, and continue mixing vigorously. Once combined, immediately pour this mixture onto your silpat or parchment paper, quickly spreading it into a single layer of peanuts, before it begins to set up. Let it cool completely before breaking into pieces. Store your brittle in an airtight container.

Makes 15 to 25 Servings

Flaming Hot Peanut Brittle

Green Tea Freezer Pops

Unabashed lover of green tea that I am, these vibrantly green freezer pops are my favorite snack to beat the heat. If you are feeling particularly indulgent, go ahead and splurge on real vanilla beans, they add amazing complexities that accentuate the matcha. To change up the taste altogether, use a pinch of lemon zest in place the vanilla for a delicious citrus twist.

1¼	Cups Plain Almond Milk
½	Cup Confectioner's Sugar
1½	Tablespoons Cornstarch
2	Teaspoons Matcha Powder
¼	Teaspoon Vanilla Extract

In a small saucepan, over medium heat, whisk together the almond milk, sugar, cornstarch, and matcha, until everything is completely dissolved. Bring the mixture up to a boil, whisking the whole time. At this point, the mixture should have thickened a bit. Remove it from the heat, stir in the vanilla, and allow it to sit for 5 minutes. Pour the mixture into ice pop molds or small paper cups. Allow it to cool for another 5 minutes, and then insert the sticks. Allow the mixture to cool to room temperature before moving the molds into the freezer, where they should sit for at least 8 hours to fully freeze.

If you have trouble getting the freezer pops out of the molds when they are ready to be eaten, simply dip the outside of the mold into a cup of warm water for a few seconds. The freezer pops should loosen enough to be easily removed.

Makes 5 to 6 Freezer Pops

Green Tea Freezer Pops

Green Tea Tiramisu

With so many wonderful desserts, I could never pick out just one recipe as my all-time favorite... that is, until I created this one. Taking a trip much further east than regular tiramisu, this version uses matcha flavoring instead of coffee, and sake rather than amaretto. Lacking vegan ladyfingers, the preparations are somewhat different, but the end results have convinced many dubious consumers that change is a good thing.

Sponge Cake:
- 1 Cup Plain Soymilk
- 1 Teaspoon Apple Cider Vinegar
- 2 Tablespoons Margarine
- 2/3 Cup Granulated Sugar
- 2 Tablespoons Canola or Vegetable Oil
- 1 Teaspoon Vanilla Extract
- 1½ Cups All-Purpose Flour
- 1 Teaspoon Baking Powder
- ½ Teaspoon Baking Soda
- ¼ Teaspoon Salt

Matcha Syrup:
- ½ Cup Water
- ¼ Cup Granulated Sugar
- ½ Cup Sake (Fermented Japanese Rice Wine)
- 1 Teaspoon Matcha Powder

Matcha Crème:
- 3 Cups Whole, Raw Cashews or 2 Cups Cashew Butter
- ¼ Cup Vegan "Sour Cream"
- ⅓ Cup Granulated Sugar
- 2 Teaspoons Matcha Powder
- 2 Tablespoons Sake (Fermented Japanese Rice Wine)
- 2 Tablespoons Maple Syrup
- 1 Teaspoon Vanilla Extract
- ¾ Cup Plain Soy Creamer

Preheat your oven to 350°F (175°C) and lightly grease an 8 x 8 inch square baking pan.

In a small bowl, combine the soymilk with the vinegar and set aside. In your stand mixer, cream together the margarine and sugar. Add in the oil and vanilla, while continuing to mix and scraping down the sides of the bowl to ensure that everything is getting incorporated. In a separate bowl, sift together the flour, baking powder, baking soda, and salt. Alternately add the dry ingredients and the now curdled soymilk into your stand mixer, and mix just until it all comes together. Be careful not to over mix. Pour the batter into your prepared pan and bake for 28 to 32 minutes, until a toothpick inserted into the center of the cake comes out clean. Let cool completely.

For the matcha syrup, bring the water to a boil in a saucepan on the stove. Add in the sugar and maintain a steady but gentle boil for 2 to 3 minutes, stirring occasionally. Remove the sugar syrup from the heat and add the sake and matcha. Whisk vigorously in order to bring the ingredients together. Let the syrup cool for at least 10 minutes.

To begin constructing your tiramisu, turn the cake out of the pan and slice it in half horizontally, so that you have two thin 8 inch squares. Use a sawing motion and a serrated knife to achieve a clean cut, and be careful when moving the layers so that they do not crumble. If they do break in half, just use the pieces together as you would have with the whole slice. Lay the two slices side by side with their cut sides up on a jelly roll pan, or any other shallow dish with walls. Pour the matcha syrup equally over both halves, being careful not to completely soak the cake, lest it become saturated and mushy. Let the cake sit and absorb while you make the crème filling.

If using whole cashews, grind them into a fine powder with your food processor. Continue to process as the nuts begin to release their natural oils and come together into a somewhat clumpy paste. In your blender or food processor, combine this freshly ground cashew butter, or your store bought version, with the "sour cream," sugar, and matcha. Blend until you get a completely smooth, creamy mixture, roughly 5 to 10 minutes. Once there are no remaining gritty bits of cashews, add in the sake, maple syrup, and vanilla, running the motor just to combine. As prepackaged cashew butter may be a bit thinner than homemade, slowly add in the creamer, until the matcha crème seems to be the right consistency.

Carefully move the bottom half of your soaked cake back into the same dish that it was baked in, so that it lies flat on the bottom. Layer half of your crème mixture evenly on top. Place the remaining cake half on top of that, and use the rest of the crème to top it off. Smooth the surface with a spatula (it will probably come right up to the top of the pan) and cover with plastic wrap. Chill for at least 2 hours, but not more than 8, as this dessert is best at its freshest.

To serve, top the whole pan with a light sprinkling of matcha, and cut into 8 equal rectangles. Enjoy with a hot cup of tea!

Makes 8 Servings

Green Tea Tiramisu

Hazelnut Ravioli

Whether you are hosting a sophisticated dinner party among friends or entertaining a romantic evening for two, this sweet finale will definitely end the event on a high note!

If working with phyllo dough isn't your cup of tea, you could easily substitute vegan wonton wrappers instead, though the end result will be quite different. Also, if you do not have a food processor handy to create your own hazelnut paste, then store bought hazelnut butter is a good alternative. Use ⅔ cup hazelnut butter in place of the 1 cup of roasted hazelnuts, and use your blender rather than a food processor when continuing on to make the hazelnut filling. Hazelnut butter can be found in natural food stores or online.

Ravioli:

1	Package Frozen Phyllo Dough
1	Cup Roasted Hazelnuts or
	⅔ Cup Hazelnut Butter
⅓	Cup Vegan "Cream Cheese"
1	Tablespoon Dutch Process Cocoa Powder
2	Teaspoons Instant Coffee Powder
1	Teaspoon Vanilla Extract
¾	Cup Confectioner's Sugar

Chocolate Sauce:

1	Cup Dark Chocolate, Chopped
¾	Cup Plain Soy Creamer
1	Teaspoon Vanilla Extract

Thaw the phyllo dough completely before beginning. Once ready, preheat your oven to 375°F (190°C) and line two baking sheets with silpats or parchment paper.

In your food processor, grind the hazelnuts for a good 5 to 10 minutes, until they break down into a smooth paste. Mix in the "cream cheese," cocoa, coffee powder, vanilla, and sugar. Blend until fully combined and fluffy.

Lay out the phyllo dough on a flat surface. Take 5 sheets at a time, and cover the rest loosely with a moist towel. Cut the rectangle of dough you are working with in half horizontally, and then in thirds vertically, so that you end up with 6 even squares. Spoon about one tablespoon of the filling into the center of a square. Lightly moisten the bottom two edges with a fingertip dipped in water, and fold the phyllo over to create a triangle. Press the edges down to make sure that there is a solid seal. Move the triangle over to a baking sheet, and repeat with each of the remaining squares. Continue taking 5 sheets or so at a time, cutting and filling them until you run out of both components. Always keep the phyllo that is not in use covered, so that it doesn't dry out. Bake the ravioli for about 10 minutes, until they become nicely browned on the surface.

To make the chocolate sauce, place the chocolate in a medium bowl. Heat the soy creamer in a microwave-safe container for about 1 minute and pour it over the chocolate. Let everything sit for about a minute, allowing the chocolate to melt, and stir until completely smooth. Fold in the vanilla. Pour the chocolate sauce into a dipping bowl, and serve warm with your ravioli.

Makes 24 to 30 Small Pastries

Hazelnut Ravioli

Matzah Toffee

Celebrating my first Passover as a vegan, I quickly discovered to my great dismay that there were absolutely no good recipes for egg-less kosher sweets. Luckily, a quick revamp of an old family favorite brought in rave reviews. Needless to say, I have been making this special treat every year since.

Matzah, to fit pan
1   Cup Margarine
1   Cup Dark Brown Sugar
12 Ounces Semi-Sweet
    Chocolate Chips

Preheat your oven to 450°F (230°C) and line a 15 x 10 inch jellyroll pan, or other shallow pan, with matzah boards. Fit them to cover the bottom evenly, without overlapping; you may need to break them to do so.

In a saucepan over medium heat, melt the margarine and brown sugar together and bring them to a slow boil. Maintain a gentle boil without stirring for 3 to 5 minutes, until the mixture becomes thick enough to coat a spoon. Pour the sugar mixture over the matzah and spread evenly. Bake in the oven for 4 minutes and remove carefully.

Sprinkle the chocolate chips on top of the matzah, then return the pan to your oven for another 30 to 60 seconds. After it comes out of the oven for this second time, gently spread the melted chocolate so that it covers the top as completely as possible.

Let the matzah toffee cool at room temperature until it has completely solidified. Break it into pieces, and store in an airtight container.

Makes 2 Pounds of Candy

Matzah Toffee

Orangettes

Few people would ever think to save an old orange peel, but when prepared correctly, they may actually make for a more delicious treat than the orange itself! It takes a little bit of effort to extract all residual bitterness from the pith, but the payoff is worth the extra work. For a simpler treat, feel free to skip the chocolate dip, but who doesn't love the combination of chocolate and orange?

3–4	Oranges
3½	Cups Water, Divided
½	Cup Granulated Sugar
3	Ounces Dark Chocolate, Chopped

There are many ways to remove the peel from the oranges. Some suggestions include using a vegetable peeler or grater, but I like to do it with a knife. To do it my way, begin by cutting the oranges into quarters. With the skin side down, cut right along the edge as close to the actual peel as possible and remove the edible innards. If there is still white pith left over on the inside of the peel, simply scrape that off with the knife. Cut the resulting clean peel into thin quarters, so that each orange produces 16 strips. You should now have a few nicely cleaned segments of orange, so take a break and have a snack, or toss them into a salad later on!

Place the cleaned strips of peel in a small saucepan and pour in enough water to cover, about 1 cup. Bring the water to a boil, and continue to cook for about 5 minutes. Drain the water, return the orange peel to the pan, and add a fresh cup of water. Bring back to a boil, cook for 5 minutes, and drain again. Repeat this process once more in order to leech out any bitterness.

Now you are ready to candy the rinds! Add the sugar and a final ½ cup of water to the peels, and boil over medium heat once more. Continue to cook until the excess water evaporates and all you have left is a thin coating of smooth sugar on each of the strips. Remove from the heat and immediately move the saucepan contents onto a silpat or parchment paper. Spread each piece out, so that they do not touch, before the sugar begins to cool and solidify. Let cool.

Once the coating has completely hardened, place the chocolate in a microwave-safe dish, and microwave in 30-second intervals to prevent scorching. Stir thoroughly after each heating until the chocolate is completely melted and smooth. Dip a piece of peel half way into the chocolate, and return it to the silpat. Repeat this process with the remaining orange peels. Allow the orangettes to dry before storing them in an airtight container.

Makes 48 to 64 Candies

Orangettes

Pumpkin Toffee Trifle

Piled with several layers of delicious flavors and served up family-style, the trifle is the epitome of unpretentious decadence, suitable for fancy dinners, holiday gatherings, or a laid-back buffet. Although it does take some patience to make each separate element, they can easily be prepared ahead of time, refrigerated, and then assembled when you are ready. If candy making is not your forte, then throw in 1 to 2 cups of chocolate chips in place of the toffee, to no ill effects.

Toffee:
¼	Cup Margarine
2	Cups Dark Brown Sugar
½	Cup Water

Pumpkin Cake:
6	Ounces Vanilla Soy Yogurt
½	Cup Granulated Sugar
½	Cup Dark Brown Sugar
1	Cup Pumpkin Purée
½	Cup Canola or Vegetable Oil
1	Teaspoon Vanilla Extract
1	Cup All-Purpose Flour
½	Cup Whole Wheat Pastry Flour
1	Teaspoon Baking Powder
1	Teaspoon Baking Soda
2	Teaspoons Ground Cinnamon
½	Teaspoon Ground Allspice
½	Teaspoon Ground Ginger
½	Teaspoon Salt
½	Teaspoon Lemon Juice

Vanilla Pudding:
3	Cups Plain Soymilk
1	Cup Plain Soy Creamer
1½	Cups Confectioner's Sugar
5	Tablespoons Cornstarch
¼	Cup Vanilla Extract

To begin making the toffee, heat the margarine, brown sugar, and water together in a large saucepan over medium heat. It is very important to stir the mixture continuously once it comes up to a boil, as it could very easily boil over if left unattended. Once rapidly bubbling, cook the sugar mixture for 12 to 15 minutes, until it reaches 300°F (150°C) or when a small amount of the mixture dropped into a cup of cold water creates hard, brittle threads. At that point, immediately pour the liquid toffee onto the centers of two large silpats or parchment paper, being careful not to pour so much that it spills over the edges. Let the mixture sit until it has completely cooled and solidified. Break the resulting toffee into bite-sized pieces and set aside.

Preheat your oven to 350°F (175°C) and lightly grease an 8 x 8 inch square baking pan.

Use a stand mixer to beat together the soy yogurt, sugars, pumpkin, oil and vanilla until everything is thoroughly combined. In a separate bowl, sift together the flours, baking powder, baking soda, spices, and salt. Slowly add these dry ingredients into the mixer, stirring just enough to bring the batter together into a smooth, homogeneous mixture. Lastly, mix in the lemon juice. Pour your batter into the prepared pan, and bake for 30 to 40 minutes. When done, the cake will pull slightly away from the sides of the pan, and it will appear to be golden brown on top. Let the cake cool completely before cutting into bite-sized cubes. Set aside.

The last component for your trifle is the vanilla pudding, which should only be prepared once all of the other parts are cooled and ready to go. Heat the soymilk and creamer in a large saucepan over medium heat. Whisk in the sugar and cornstarch while still relatively cool, dissolving all of the particles. Keep stirring gently while the temperature increases and the starch begins to swell. When you start to feel the liquid thickening, quicken your pace in stirring, and continue to cook for up to 5 minutes, until it takes on the consistency of a thin pudding. It will thicken further as it cools. Remove the mixture from the heat, stir in the vanilla, and keep agitating it for a few additional minutes. Wait for the pudding to cool completely before assembling the trifle, or you will melt the toffee!

To put everything together, place half of the cake cubes in a trifle dish, in as even a layer as possible. Top this with half of the pudding, and then half of the broken toffee pieces. The rest of the cake follows, continuing the same pattern with the rest of the pudding on top of that, and the remainder of the toffee to finish. If you don't plan on serving it immediately, cover the dish with plastic wrap before storing it in the refrigerator. Serve within 24 hours.

Makes 15 to 20 Servings

Pumpkin Toffee Trifle

Sesame Chews

These chewy candies were born out of sheer luck. Playing around in the kitchen one day with various sugars and add-ins left over from previous baking ventures, I had no idea what might result from the pot bubbling away on my stove. Luckily, the results were not some strange science experiment to be discarded at the end of the day, but rather a tasty, toothsome treat! An unusual flavor sensation to be sure, you might be surprised how well the ingredients play together in this unique sweet.

¼	Cup Granulated Sugar
¾	Cup Dark Agave Nectar
¾	Cup Sesame Seeds
½	Cup Sliced Almonds
½	Teaspoon Vanilla Extract
¼	Teaspoon Baking Soda

Line an 8 x 8 inch square baking pan with parchment paper or aluminum foil, and grease well.

In a medium saucepan, heat the sugar and agave nectar together slowly, until the sugar is dissolved and the mixture comes to a boil. Add in your seeds and nuts, and mix continuously while cooking for 4 to 5 minutes. When the mixture has thickened slightly, remove the pan from the stove. Add in the vanilla and baking soda, stirring vigorously until everything is combined and the candy has lightened slightly in color and texture.

Pour the liquid candy into your prepared baking pan and resist the urge to spread it out manually. Once it goes into the pan, do not touch it for at least 30 minutes. After that time has elapsed, move it into the refrigerator to finish setting up, for about an hour. To cut the chews, remove them from the foil and use a heavy knife that is long enough to cover the whole length that you are slicing. Press straight down, rocking the knife back and forth if it needs more persuasion, but do not saw.

The chews may stick together due to humidity; so it is best to separate the layers with parchment paper. Store them in an airtight container in a cool place.

Makes 24 to 32 Chews

Sesame Chews

Trigona

Appeasing my father's sweet tooth has always been a challenge. While he loves sugar in its most pure and concentrated form, and appreciates candies of all types, traditional desserts do not really do it for him. If one exception could be made, however, it would be for baklava. Unfortunately, as his birthday fast approached, my plans to make him baklava hit a bump in the road when I had neglected to obtain the proper ingredients. Luckily, some fast thinking saved the day. While it utilizes pistachios instead of walnuts and maple syrup instead of the traditional honey in baklava, trigona is a very similar dessert in assembly and concept. This generous helping of sweet, crunchy, and spicy was completely devoured within a single day, and it earned an enthusiastic seal of approval from my picky father.

1	Package Frozen Phyllo Dough
16	Ounces Shelled Pistachios
½	Cup Granulated Sugar
1	Teaspoon Ground Cinnamon
1	Cup Margarine, Melted
1½	Cups Maple Syrup

Thaw the phyllo dough completely before beginning. Once ready, preheat your oven to 300°F (150°C) and lightly grease a 9 x 13 inch baking pan.

Very briefly process the pistachios in your blender or food processor to get a coarse grind, but be sure that they are still very rough and chunky. In a separate bowl, mix together the ground pistachios, sugar, and cinnamon.

Cut (or tear) the phyllo so that it will fit into the bottom of your prepared baking pan. It is okay if the pieces overlap a little. Begin by laying down one sheet and brushing the pastry with melted margarine. Add another sheet of phyllo once the first is lightly but thoroughly coated. Brush the second sheet with margarine. Repeat these steps up to 4 times to create a phyllo layer; the exact number is up to you. After applying the margarine to the last sheet in your first phyllo layer, sprinkle it evenly with the nut mixture. Repeat the entire process to create a second layer of phyllo, followed by another layer of the nuts. Continue this pattern until you run out of the dry ingredients, and end with a layer of nuts on the top.

Before placing the trigona in the oven, pre-cut the little triangles, or, if you are not feeling so handy with a knife, little squares are just fine. Bake for 70 to 80 minutes, until golden brown and slightly crispy-looking, but watch to make sure that the nuts do not burn!

Gently warm the maple syrup, either over the stove or in the microwave, and pour it over the baked pastry. Allow the trigona to cool for at least one hour, re-cut, and serve.

Makes 24 Triangles

Trigona

Food Allergy Index

Strawberry Love Muffins	30
Strawberry Spirals	72
Sweet & Simple French Toast	32
Trigona	178
Triple Threat Chocolate ""Cheese"" Cake	126
Turtle Shortbread Wedges	74
Wasabi Chocolate Cupcakes	128
Whoopie Pies	76
Zesty Cranberry Crumb Muffins	34

Tree Nut Free*

Bananas Foster Cake	82
Black & Whites	42
Black Bottom Blondies	44
Brilliant Berry Parfaits	154
Butterscotch Blondies	46
Canine Cake	84
Caramel Macchiato "Cheese" Cake	86
Chai "Cheese" Cake	88
"Cheese" Cake Thumbprint Cookies	48
Cherry Chocolate Truffles	156
Chocolate Chip Cookie Pie	138
Chocolate-Glazed Peanut Butter Scones	18
Cocoa Crumble	158
Coconut Custard Pie	140
Coffee Break Shortbread	50
Cookies and Crème Pound Cake	90
Crumb-Topped Brownies	52
Dried Fruit Focaccia	20
Five-Minute Coconut Fudge	160
Flaming Hot Peanut Brittle	162
Golden Glazed Donuts	22
Graham Flour Fig Scones	24
Lace Sugar Crisps	54
Lemon-Lime Sunshine Bundt	94
Lychee Cupcakes with Raspberry Frosting	96
Marshmallow Mud Cake	98
Matzah Toffee	170
Mini Icebox "Cheese" Cake	100
Mocha Devastation Cake	102
Oatmeal Raisin Rolls	26
Orange Dreamsicle Snack Cake	106
Orangettes	172
Peach Melba Layer Cake	108
Peanut Butter Bombs	64
Peanut-Plus Cookies	66

Piña Colada Mini-Bundts	110
Pink Lemonade Tartlets	148
Plum-Good Crumb Cake	112
Pomegranate Ginger Cupcakes	114
Poppy Seed Cupcakes with Lemon Curd Filling	116
Pumpkin Toffee Trifle	174
Root Beer Float Cupcakes	120
Self-Frosting Peanut Butter Cupcakes	122
Sesame Oatmeal Cookies	70
Strawberry Love Muffins	30
Strawberry Spirals	72
Sweet & Simple French Toast	32
Triple Threat Chocolate ""Cheese"" Cake	126
Wasabi Chocolate Cupcakes	128
Whoopie Pies	76
Zesty Cranberry Crumb Muffins	34

Soy-Free*

Better Banana Nut Muffins**	16
Canine Cake	84
Dried Fruit Focaccia	20
Flaming Hot Peanut Brittle	162
Green Tea Freezer Pops	164
Orangettes	172
Peanut-Plus Cookies**	66
Pomegranate Ginger Cupcakes**	114
Root Beer Float Cupcakes**	120
Self-Frosting Peanut Butter Cupcakes**	122
Sesame Chews	176
Sesame Oatmeal Cookies**	70
Strawberry Love Muffins**	30
Sweet & Simple French Toast**	32
Wasabi Chocolate Cupcakes**	128

Several of my recipes contain margarine as the only known soy-based ingredient. While there are a few brands of soy-free margarine and shortening available internationally, I have not specifically trialed them in these recipes, and thus hesitate to recommend the swap. However, feel free to experiment if you are seeking more soy-free options.

* Always check that the ingredients you are purchasing are safe for the food allergy or sensitivity in question. While I can note which recipes do not contain a particular allergen ingredient to the best of my knowledge, it is always up to the consumer to verify ingredients and any potential cross-contamination issues.

** Feel free to substitute the soymilk in this recipe with your favorite soy-free milk alternative, such as rice, almond, or hemp milk.

Ingredient Index

Metric Conversions

Liquid / Dry Measures

U.S.	Metric
¼ teaspoon	1.25 milliliters
½ teaspoon	2.5 milliliters
1 teaspoon	5 milliliters
1 tablespoon	15 milliliters
1 fluid ounce	30 milliliters
¼ cup	60 milliliters
⅓ cup	80 milliliters
½ cup	120 milliliters
1 cup	240 milliliters
1 pint (2 cups)	480 milliliters
1 quart (4 cups)	960 milliliters
1 ounce (by weight)	28 grams
4 ounces (by weight)	113 grams
16 ounces (1 pound)	454 grams

Baking Pans

U.S.	Metric	Metric Volume
8 x 8 inch	20 x 20 centimeters	2 Liters
9 x 13 inch	23 x 33 centimeters	3.5 Liters
9 x 5 inch (loaf)	23 x 13 centimeters	2 Liters
12 x 17 inch	30 x 43 centimeters	
4 x 13 inch	10 x 33 centimeters	
8 inch round (cake)	20 x 4 centimeters	1.2 Liters
9 inch round (cake)	23 x 4 centimeters	1.5 Liters
9 inch round (pie)	23 x 3 centimeters	1 Liter
6 inch round (springform)	15 centimeter round	
9 inch round (springform)	23 centimeter round	
10 inch round (bundt)	25 centimeter round	

Length

U.S.	Metric
⅛ inch	3 millimeters
¼ inch	6 millimeters
½ inch	12 millimeters
1 inch	2.5 centimeters